The Food and Beverage Industry Handbook

A Complete Guide to Success

Table of Contents

Chapter 1: Introduction to the Food and Beverage Industry	4
Chapter 2: The History of Food and Beverage	11
Chapter 3: Types of Food and Beverage Businesses	19
Chapter 4: Supply Chain in Food and Beverage	26
Chapter 5: Food Safety and Quality Standards	33
Chapter 6: Menu Planning and Development	40
Chapter 7: Kitchen Operations and Equipment	46
Chapter 8: Beverage Operations and Management	53
Chapter 9: Food and Beverage Service Standards	60
Chapter 10: Staff Training and Development	67
Chapter 11: Health and Nutrition in Food and Beverage	75
Chapter 12: Marketing and Branding for Food and Beverage Businesses	83
Chapter 13: Financial Management in Food and Beverage	91
Chapter 14: Food and Beverage Technology Trends	98
Chapter 15: Sustainability in the Food and Beverage Industry	105
Chapter 16: Franchising and Expansion in Food and Beverage	111
Chapter 17: Legal and Regulatory Compliance	118
Chapter 18: Trends in the Food and Beverage Industry	124
Chapter 19: Event Catering and Special Services	132
Chapter 20: Customer Experience in Food and Beverage	139
Chapter 21: Crisis Management in Food and Beverage	146
Chapter 22: Emerging Technologies and Innovations	153
Chapter 23: Food and Beverage Entrepreneurship	160
Chapter 24: Case Studies of Successful Food and Beverage Brands	167
Chapter 25: Future of the Food and Beverage Industry	174

Chapter 1: Introduction to the Food and Beverage Industry

The Food and Beverage (F&B) industry is one of the most essential and dynamic sectors of the global economy. It encompasses a wide array of activities, from the farming and production of raw ingredients to the preparation, packaging, distribution, and serving of food and beverages to consumers. As a vital part of human life and culture, the industry's operations touch everyone, influencing social, cultural, and economic landscapes worldwide. This chapter offers an overview of the F&B industry, highlighting its economic importance, its impact on global markets, and its various key sectors.

Overview of the Industry

The Food and Beverage industry includes multiple sub-sectors dedicated to the production, distribution, and sale of food and drink. The value chain begins with raw material production (agriculture, livestock, fisheries) and extends through food processing, packaging, distribution, and retail. At its core, the F&B industry provides essential sustenance to the global population, but it also goes beyond basic nourishment to include elements of culture, convenience, entertainment, and even lifestyle.

This industry operates at both small and large scales, from independent restaurants and small-scale food producers to multinational corporations. In recent decades, technological advances, globalization, and shifting consumer preferences have driven transformative changes across the industry. The introduction of automation, data analytics, and e-commerce has streamlined production and expanded consumer access, making F&B goods more widely available and enhancing service delivery.

The global nature of the industry has led to significant interdependencies between countries, with raw materials, processed products, and services often crossing international borders. This international reach allows for a diverse selection of products for consumers but also introduces complexities, such as food safety concerns, supply chain issues, and the environmental impact of food production and distribution.

Importance and Impact on the Global Economy

The Food and Beverage industry plays a pivotal role in the global economy. It is a major contributor to Gross Domestic Product (GDP) in many countries, accounting for substantial portions of both employment and trade. The industry supports millions of jobs globally, ranging from farming and food processing to retail and service roles. In developed nations, the F&B industry is typically one of the largest employment sectors. In emerging economies, it is often the backbone of the labor market, particularly in rural areas where agriculture is a dominant activity.

Economic Contributions: The Food and Beverage sector contributes billions of dollars to the global economy each year. In many nations, it accounts for a significant portion of GDP. The industry is deeply interconnected with other economic sectors, including agriculture, transportation, retail, and hospitality. Each of these sectors supports F&B through the supply of raw materials, logistics, sales, and service, which in turn creates a ripple effect across economies. Furthermore, the industry is integral to the economies of countries that rely heavily on agricultural exports. For example, economies in Latin America, Africa, and Asia depend on exports of coffee, cocoa, grains, and spices, which are critical components of the F&B market.

Employment Generation: Employment in the F&B industry spans a wide range of skill levels, from agricultural and factory workers to chefs, waitstaff, marketers, and product developers. According to industry reports, the sector employs over a billion people globally, making it one of the largest employment providers. This vast employment base helps reduce poverty and supports family incomes, particularly in rural regions and developing countries where agricultural work is common. Additionally, the hospitality aspect of the industry (restaurants, cafes, and catering) is a significant job provider in urban areas, attracting people with various skill levels and educational backgrounds.

Trade and Exports: The Food and Beverage industry is highly influential in the global trade landscape. Agricultural exports, processed food, and beverages flow across borders, meeting demand in regions that cannot locally produce certain products due to climate, geography, or resource limitations. Countries that specialize in certain foods, such as wine from France, cheese from Switzerland, and chocolate from Belgium, find lucrative markets worldwide. The sector's reliance on international trade has also led to the development of regulations and standards that ensure food safety, sustainability, and ethical sourcing practices across global supply chains.

Investment and Innovation: Due to its scale and diversity, the Food and Beverage industry attracts substantial investment, both from private and public sectors. Investments in research and development (R&D) drive innovation, resulting in new products, improved food safety measures, and enhanced production methods. Innovations in food processing, packaging, and preservation have extended product shelf life and expanded distribution options, making it possible to serve remote markets. Investments in F&B technology, particularly in areas like alternative proteins, plant-based foods, and sustainable packaging, reflect the industry's adaptability to changing consumer expectations for healthier and environmentally friendly products.

Key Sectors within Food and Beverage

The Food and Beverage industry is comprised of various key sectors, each playing a unique role in the production, distribution, and service of food and beverages. Understanding these sectors is essential for grasping the complexity of the industry as a whole.

Restaurants and Food Service Establishments: Restaurants, cafes, and food trucks make up one of the most visible segments of the F&B industry. These establishments offer a wide range of cuisines and dining experiences, from quick-service and fast food to fine dining. The sector is highly competitive and driven by changing consumer preferences for dining experiences that balance quality, convenience, and value. Recently, restaurants have adapted to trends such as online ordering, food delivery, and "ghost kitchens" (kitchens that prepare food exclusively for delivery), expanding their reach and accessibility.

Catering and Events: Catering services provide food for events, such as weddings, corporate functions, and private gatherings. Catering businesses are unique because they must ensure food quality while adapting to various event settings, often transporting food to different locations. This sector demands flexibility and efficiency to meet the needs of diverse clients and to cater to large-scale gatherings. With the rise of customized and experiential dining, catering has evolved to offer specialized services like themed events, live cooking stations, and tailored menus.

Food Manufacturing and Processing: Food manufacturing is one of the largest sectors in the industry, encompassing the processing of raw ingredients into products for consumer and industrial use. This includes everything from canning, freezing, and baking to the production of snack foods, dairy products, beverages, and condiments. Food processing often requires large-scale operations and advanced machinery to ensure efficiency, quality, and food safety. This sector is also central to food innovation, introducing new product types, flavors, and formats to meet the demands of consumers who seek both convenience and novel experiences.

Retail Food and Beverage: Retail food encompasses grocery stores, supermarkets, convenience stores, and specialty food shops. This sector serves as the primary source of food for consumers purchasing ingredients for home preparation. The retail sector has seen rapid changes with the advent of online shopping and grocery delivery services, which allow consumers to shop for groceries from the convenience of their homes. Specialty food retailers also cater to niche markets, such as organic, vegan, or locally sourced products, capitalizing on growing demand for diverse and health-conscious options.

Beverage Industry: The beverage sector includes the production and sale of alcoholic and non-alcoholic drinks. Non-alcoholic beverages encompass soft drinks, bottled water, juices, teas, and coffees, while alcoholic beverages include beer, wine, spirits, and craft drinks. The beverage sector is continually evolving, with new products and brands emerging to meet shifting consumer tastes. For example, there is a growing market for healthy beverages like kombucha and cold-pressed juices, as well as innovative options like low-alcohol and alcohol-free drinks. Similarly, the craft beverage movement has led to the rise of microbreweries and small-scale distilleries.

Agriculture and Raw Material Production: The agriculture sector serves as the foundation of the Food and Beverage industry by supplying raw ingredients such as grains, fruits, vegetables, meat, and dairy. Farmers and producers play an essential role in the food chain, often operating within specific climatic conditions or geographic areas suited to particular crops or livestock. Agriculture also relies heavily on technology, with advancements in precision farming, irrigation systems, and crop genetics improving yields and sustainability. Challenges in this sector, including climate change and water scarcity, have increased the focus on sustainable and resilient agricultural practices.

Logistics and Distribution: Efficient logistics and distribution are essential to the F&B industry's success, ensuring that products move from production facilities to retail stores and restaurants. The logistics sector includes warehousing, transportation, and inventory management, all of which contribute to the timely delivery of perishable goods. Cold chain logistics, which involves temperature-controlled storage and transport, is especially critical for preserving food quality and safety. With the growth of e-commerce, logistics has expanded to include last-mile delivery solutions, making it easier for consumers to access fresh and packaged foods at their doorstep.

The Food and Beverage industry is a multifaceted sector with a significant impact on the global economy, encompassing everything from agriculture and food processing to restaurants and logistics. Its influence extends far beyond the products it sells, shaping employment, culture, and economic activity worldwide. With its variety of sectors, this industry provides consumers with essential products and services, while also adapting to new trends, innovations, and challenges. By understanding the structure and significance of the F&B industry, stakeholders can better appreciate its contributions and anticipate the future trends that will continue to reshape it. This foundation is crucial for delving deeper into the specific sectors and operations that make the industry as vast and dynamic as it is.

Chapter 2: The History of Food and Beverage

The history of the Food and Beverage (F&B) industry is as old as human civilization itself. From the moment humans began gathering and preparing food, the industry started its evolutionary journey. Throughout millennia, the ways food and beverages are produced, distributed, and consumed have seen significant shifts. This chapter explores the major milestones in the evolution of the F&B industry, examining the profound influences of culture, technology, and trade that have shaped it into the complex, global network it is today.

Evolution of the Industry Over Time

The F&B industry has progressed through several stages, each marked by pivotal changes in how food is sourced, prepared, and served. Key historical developments offer insights into how early practices have laid the groundwork for today's vast and diversified industry.

Prehistoric and Ancient Times: In prehistoric times, early humans were hunter-gatherers, relying on wild plants and animals for sustenance. The domestication of plants and animals around 10,000 BCE marked a transformative period, allowing humans to transition to settled agricultural communities. This shift led to food surplus, which spurred population growth and gave rise to the first civilizations.

Ancient cultures such as the Egyptians, Greeks, and Romans began developing sophisticated agricultural techniques, such as irrigation and crop rotation. These societies produced food not just for survival, but also for trade and social ceremonies, laying the foundation for food as a form of cultural expression and exchange.

Middle Ages: The Middle Ages witnessed further developments, particularly in Europe, where the feudal system influenced agriculture. During this period, monasteries played a vital role in preserving agricultural knowledge and food production techniques. Monks cultivated vineyards and brewed beer, laying the foundation for European wine and brewing traditions that continue today.

Additionally, the spread of Islam fostered agricultural innovation across the Middle East and North Africa. Islamic scholars introduced new crops and irrigation methods to Europe, including staples like rice, citrus fruits, and sugarcane, further enriching the diversity of food production.

The Age of Exploration: The Age of Exploration (15th to 17th centuries) brought about significant changes in food and beverage through the establishment of global trade networks. European explorers introduced New World crops, such as tomatoes, potatoes, maize, and cocoa, to the Old World. Similarly, they brought European goods, such as wheat and sugar, to the Americas. These exchanges, often referred to as the "Columbian Exchange," revolutionized diets and agricultural practices on both sides of the Atlantic.

This era also saw the rise of colonial plantations that produced high-demand crops like sugar, coffee, and tea. These products quickly became staples in Europe and led to the development of global trade routes, which influenced culinary practices and created a new economic dependence on imported goods.

Industrial Revolution: The Industrial Revolution of the 18th and 19th centuries was a defining period for the F&B industry. Technological advances, such as the steam engine and mechanized farming equipment, greatly increased agricultural productivity and food processing capabilities. Innovations like canning, refrigeration, and pasteurization transformed food storage, making it possible to preserve food for longer periods and transport it over vast distances.

This era also saw the growth of large food factories and the beginnings of mass production in food and beverage. As cities grew, urban populations increasingly relied on industrialized food production, giving rise to modern food manufacturing. Consumer demand for affordable, readily available food items paved the way for products like canned goods, processed cereals, and bottled beverages.

20th Century – Rise of Convenience and Fast Food: The 20th century marked the rise of convenience foods and the global spread of fast food. After World War II, technological advances such as freeze-drying and microwaveable packaging made it easier to produce, store, and prepare food quickly. The fast-food industry emerged during this period, with franchises like McDonald's and KFC becoming household names across the world.

This period also saw the introduction of processed foods, snacks, and ready-to-eat meals. As lifestyles grew busier, consumer preferences shifted toward food options that prioritized speed and convenience, significantly influencing the structure of the industry.

21st Century – Health, Sustainability, and Innovation: In the 21st century, the F&B industry is increasingly influenced by health, sustainability, and technological innovation. Consumers have become more health-conscious, driving demand for organic, plant-based, and low-calorie options. Sustainability has also become a priority, with companies adopting eco-friendly packaging, waste reduction practices, and sourcing ethically.

Advances in technology have opened new possibilities, such as food delivery apps, digital ordering, and the use of artificial intelligence in product development and customer service. Plant-based meats, lab-grown proteins, and other innovative food alternatives reflect the industry's ability to adapt to evolving consumer demands.

Key Milestones in Food and Beverage Development

The F&B industry has experienced transformative milestones, each bringing new practices, products, and global reach.

Domestication of Plants and Animals: The shift from hunting and gathering to agriculture allowed humans to establish permanent settlements. This development fostered stable food supplies and set the stage for organized food production and storage.

Invention of Fermentation and Preservation: Early humans discovered fermentation, using it to make alcoholic beverages and preserve foods. The ability to preserve food was essential for survival, especially in areas where seasonal changes affected food availability.

Rise of Food Markets and Trade Routes: The establishment of food markets and trade routes allowed for the exchange of goods, spices, and cooking techniques between different regions. Markets in ancient Rome, Greece, and China became central to commerce and cultural exchange, creating a more interconnected world.

Development of Food Safety and Preservation Techniques: The Industrial Revolution brought technological advancements that improved food safety and storage, such as canning and pasteurization. These innovations reduced spoilage and made it possible to safely transport food over longer distances.

Introduction of Fast Food and Chain Restaurants: The post-WWII era saw the growth of fast food and chain restaurants, which standardized food production and service. This model became globally popular, setting the foundation for multinational fast-food corporations that operate across continents.

Digital Transformation and E-commerce: In recent years, digital platforms have revolutionized food service and retail, enabling consumers to order food online, use delivery services, and access a vast array of dining options with ease. Digital ordering, virtual kitchens, and online grocery shopping have reshaped the consumer experience.

Influences of Culture, Technology, and Trade

The evolution of the F&B industry has been shaped by several influential factors: culture, technology, and trade.

Culture: Food and beverage have always been closely tied to cultural identity. The ingredients, flavors, and cooking techniques of a region reflect its geography, climate, and history. For instance, Mediterranean cuisine incorporates olive oil, garlic, and fresh vegetables due to the region's climate, while Asian cuisines have relied on rice, soy, and fish due to local availability.

Cultural exchange has enriched the F&B industry, introducing people to a variety of cuisines. Globalization has made dishes from diverse cultures accessible worldwide, fostering a cosmopolitan dining culture where fusion cuisines blend different culinary traditions.

Technology: Technological advancements have driven profound changes in the F&B industry. Early innovations, such as fire and clay pots, allowed for the preparation of cooked food. As technology advanced, developments in food processing, refrigeration, and packaging enabled food to be preserved, transported, and consumed in new ways. The 20th century introduced machines that could mass-produce food products, making them affordable and widely available.

In recent years, technology has introduced innovations like genetically modified organisms (GMOs), automated food processing, and digital ordering systems. Technology not only enhances production and service efficiency but also enables customized consumer experiences, such as apps for tracking dietary preferences and nutritional information.

Trade: Trade has been a driving force in the globalization of the F&B industry. Ancient trade routes, such as the Silk Road, facilitated the exchange of spices, grains, and beverages between Asia, Europe, and the Middle East. These exchanges broadened culinary horizons and introduced spices, teas, and exotic ingredients to new regions.

In the modern era, global supply chains have expanded the availability of diverse foods and beverages. However, this interdependence also introduces challenges, such as the environmental cost of transportation and the need for rigorous quality standards across different regions. Trade regulations, tariffs, and agreements continue to influence the flow of food products between nations, impacting both availability and pricing.

The history of the Food and Beverage industry is a testament to human ingenuity, adaptability, and cultural exchange. From the early days of agriculture and fermentation to today's digital platforms and sustainable practices, the F&B industry has continuously evolved to meet the needs and preferences of society. Key milestones, such as the rise of agriculture, global trade routes, industrialization, and digital innovation, have not only expanded food options but also made the industry a cornerstone of the global economy. Cultural, technological, and trade influences have each played a pivotal role in shaping the industry, ensuring that food remains not only a necessity but also a powerful symbol of identity, community, and progress.

Chapter 3: Types of Food and Beverage Businesses

The Food and Beverage (F&B) industry encompasses a wide range of businesses, each catering to unique customer preferences, experiences, and needs. This chapter delves into the primary types of F&B businesses, including restaurants (fine dining, casual, and fast-food), bars, cafes, coffee shops, food processing and manufacturing, as well as grocery and retail food services. Understanding these business types provides insight into the diversity of the industry and highlights the specific roles each type plays in the food ecosystem.

1. Restaurants

Restaurants are perhaps the most recognizable and varied segment of the F&B industry. They provide spaces where patrons can enjoy prepared meals and beverages in an environment designed to offer comfort, ambiance, and often, a social experience. The restaurant segment includes several categories, each distinguished by its menu offerings, price points, service styles, and target customer base.

Fine Dining: Fine dining restaurants offer high-end, sophisticated experiences with an emphasis on exceptional service, gourmet cuisine, and elegant ambiance. These establishments often serve carefully curated dishes made with premium ingredients, typically prepared by highly trained chefs. Menus at fine dining venues frequently change to reflect seasonal ingredients, and the service staff is expected to be knowledgeable about both the food and wine pairings. Fine dining is synonymous with luxury and exclusivity, catering to customers who seek an elevated dining experience and are willing to pay for it. Common features include multi-course meals, impeccable table settings, and attentive service that prioritizes customer comfort and satisfaction.

Casual Dining: Casual dining restaurants occupy a middle ground between fine dining and fast food. They offer moderately priced meals in a relaxed atmosphere, often catering to families, friends, and groups looking for a social yet informal dining experience. The menus in casual dining establishments tend to be broad, with familiar dishes such as burgers, pasta, salads, and grilled items. Chain restaurants such as Olive Garden and Applebee's are examples of casual dining, as they provide consistent, reliable food quality across locations while maintaining a welcoming environment. Service at casual dining restaurants is attentive but less formal than in fine dining.

Fast Food: Fast food restaurants focus on providing affordable, quick meals in a standardized format. These establishments operate on high-volume service models, with streamlined menus that prioritize efficiency and convenience. The popularity of fast food can be attributed to its low cost, convenience, and consistency. Menu items are generally simple, such as burgers, fries, chicken sandwiches, and pizza. Unlike fine or casual dining, fast food is often designed for takeaway or drive-thru service. McDonald's, Burger King, and KFC are iconic examples of fast food chains that have become globally recognized for their speed, affordability, and branding.

2. Bars, Cafes, and Coffee Shops

Bars, cafes, and coffee shops are important parts of the F&B industry, each providing unique environments for social interaction and relaxation. These establishments focus on beverages as the primary product, though many also offer light food options to complement the drinks.

Bars: Bars are establishments primarily focused on serving alcoholic beverages, though they may also offer a selection of non-alcoholic drinks and snacks. Bars are social spaces where patrons gather to unwind, socialize, and enjoy crafted cocktails, beer, and wine. Different types of bars include pubs, wine bars, cocktail bars, and sports bars, each catering to specific clientele and offering distinct ambiance and menu options. Pubs, for example, often serve traditional comfort food alongside beer, while wine bars feature curated wine lists paired with appetizers or small plates. Bars are often hubs for nightlife and entertainment, frequently featuring live music, DJs, or sporting event broadcasts.

Cafes and Coffee Shops: Cafes and coffee shops are spaces that emphasize coffee, tea, and light snacks. Cafes have a long-standing cultural significance, originating in Europe and eventually spreading worldwide as centers for socialization and relaxation. Coffee shops like Starbucks have modernized this tradition, offering specialty coffee drinks, pastries, sandwiches, and a cozy ambiance that encourages patrons to linger. The setting in cafes and coffee shops is generally relaxed, often featuring comfortable seating, Wi-Fi access, and a welcoming atmosphere where customers can work, read, or socialize. Independent coffee shops often add unique character to communities by promoting local culture, offering specialty roasts, and supporting sustainable sourcing practices.

3. Food Processing and Manufacturing

Food processing and manufacturing form a critical component of the F&B industry, encompassing all activities involved in transforming raw ingredients into packaged and market-ready food products. This sector plays a vital role in ensuring that food is safe, nutritious, and accessible on a large scale.

Food Processing: Food processing refers to the methods used to transform raw ingredients into consumable products. Processes include canning, freezing, drying, pasteurizing, and packaging, which extend the shelf life of food and enhance its safety. Processed foods range from canned vegetables and dairy products to ready-to-eat meals and snacks.

Food processing companies work within stringent regulatory frameworks to meet safety and quality standards. The sector includes a variety of players, from large corporations that produce popular consumer brands to smaller producers specializing in organic or artisanal products.

Food Manufacturing: Food manufacturing builds on processing by producing packaged, branded food items ready for retail distribution. Companies in food manufacturing produce a wide array of products, including breakfast cereals, dairy products, baked goods, confectionery, beverages, and more. Some manufacturers focus on health-oriented products, such as gluten-free or low-sugar options, to meet consumer demand for healthy eating. Large multinational companies, such as Nestlé, PepsiCo, and Unilever, dominate the food manufacturing industry and have global supply chains to support their extensive production and distribution networks.

Innovation and Technology in Food Manufacturing: Technological advancements have had a major impact on food manufacturing, enabling greater efficiency, quality control, and innovation. Automated production lines, robotics, and data-driven processes have streamlined manufacturing operations, allowing for mass production without compromising on quality. Additionally, technology has enabled new categories of food products, such as plant-based meat alternatives and functional foods that offer health benefits beyond basic nutrition.

4. Grocery and Retail Food Services

Grocery and retail food services encompass the final stage in the F&B supply chain, where food products reach consumers. This category includes supermarkets, specialty food stores, and e-commerce platforms that provide fresh produce, packaged goods, and ready-to-eat meals.

Supermarkets and Grocery Stores: Supermarkets and grocery stores are integral to daily life, offering a vast selection of food products and household essentials. They are known for their convenience, variety, and competitive pricing. Supermarkets typically feature fresh produce, meat, dairy, and frozen foods, alongside packaged and prepared foods. In recent years, supermarkets have adapted to consumer preferences by adding organic, locally-sourced, and health-focused options. Large chains, such as Walmart and Kroger, offer one-stop shopping experiences that cater to diverse consumer needs.

Specialty Food Stores: Specialty food stores focus on niche markets, such as organic, gourmet, ethnic, or health foods. These stores often appeal to consumers who prioritize quality, artisanal craftsmanship, or unique ingredients. Specialty stores like Whole Foods Market and Trader Joe's are popular in the U.S. for offering organic products and foods sourced from around the world. Specialty stores have smaller footprints than traditional supermarkets and often emphasize high-quality or unique products over sheer volume.

E-commerce and Online Grocery: Online grocery shopping has grown rapidly, especially with the convenience it offers in today's fast-paced world. E-commerce platforms allow consumers to order groceries and prepared foods from the comfort of their homes, often with same-day delivery options. Services like Amazon Fresh, Instacart, and Walmart's online grocery delivery have expanded access to fresh food and household items. The COVID-19 pandemic accelerated the shift to online grocery shopping, making it a preferred choice for many consumers and prompting retailers to enhance their digital infrastructure.

The F&B industry comprises a wide range of business models, each meeting the diverse needs of consumers for nutrition, convenience, and social engagement. Restaurants provide settings that range from luxurious to quick-service, catering to various dining preferences. Bars, cafes, and coffee shops create social environments centered around beverages, while food processing and manufacturing ensure that a steady supply of packaged goods is available for retail. Grocery and retail food services bring these goods to the end consumer, making food products accessible and affordable across different markets.

Each type of F&B business has a distinct role, contributing to the industry's overall complexity and adaptability. The continued evolution of these businesses in response to consumer demands, technological advances, and market dynamics ensures that the F&B industry remains one of the most dynamic and resilient sectors globally.

Chapter 4: Supply Chain in Food and Beverage

The supply chain in the Food and Beverage (F&B) industry is a highly intricate and essential process, encompassing everything from sourcing ingredients and raw materials to managing inventory, procurement, distribution, and logistics. Effective supply chain management in this industry is vital to ensure the timely availability of high-quality ingredients, the freshness of perishable goods, and the efficiency of delivery systems. In this chapter, we will explore the key elements of supply chain management specific to the F&B sector: sourcing ingredients, distribution and logistics, and inventory management and procurement.

1. Sourcing Ingredients and Raw Materials

The sourcing of ingredients and raw materials is the foundational stage in the F&B supply chain, as it directly influences the quality, safety, and sustainability of the final product. In a globalized market, F&B companies often source materials from various regions to obtain the best quality and cost-effective options, but this comes with unique challenges.

Local vs. Global Sourcing: Sourcing can be local, where ingredients are obtained from nearby farms and suppliers, or global, where materials are imported from distant regions. Local sourcing can improve freshness, reduce transportation costs, and appeal to consumers interested in supporting local economies. However, it may limit access to certain ingredients only available in specific climates or regions. Global sourcing, on the other hand, allows companies to access a wide variety of ingredients year-round but can complicate logistics and increase transportation costs. F&B companies must weigh these options carefully based on their product requirements and consumer preferences.

Sustainable and Ethical Sourcing: With growing consumer demand for transparency and ethical practices, many F&B businesses prioritize sustainable sourcing, including fair trade certifications, organic production, and environmentally friendly farming practices. This approach helps ensure that sourcing practices protect natural resources, promote fair labor practices, and reduce carbon footprints. For example, many coffee and cocoa brands partner with fair trade-certified suppliers to ensure equitable pay and safe working conditions for farmers. Sustainable sourcing is increasingly critical for brand reputation and customer loyalty.

Supplier Relationships and Quality Assurance: The quality and consistency of ingredients are paramount in the F&B industry. Companies often establish long-term relationships with trusted suppliers to maintain high standards and ensure the reliability of their supply chains. Contracts and service-level agreements (SLAs) with suppliers often include specific quality standards, delivery timelines, and contingency plans to handle disruptions. Moreover, companies may implement quality assurance programs, including regular audits, sampling, and testing of raw materials, to verify supplier compliance and protect against risks such as contamination or adulteration.

2. Distribution and Logistics

Efficient distribution and logistics are critical in the F&B supply chain, especially given the perishability of many food products. F&B companies rely on robust logistics systems to move ingredients and finished products from suppliers to production facilities, distribution centers, and, ultimately, to retailers or end consumers. Ensuring timely, safe, and cost-effective distribution requires meticulous planning and coordination.

Cold Chain Logistics: Cold chain logistics involves a temperature-controlled supply chain that is essential for transporting perishable goods such as dairy, meat, seafood, and fresh produce.

Maintaining optimal temperatures from the source to the destination prevents spoilage and extends shelf life, which is crucial for quality and safety. The cold chain requires specialized refrigerated storage, trucks, containers, and handling procedures. Advances in cold chain technology, such as GPS and IoT-enabled sensors, allow companies to monitor temperature and humidity in real-time, ensuring products arrive in optimal condition.

Last-Mile Delivery: The last-mile delivery phase is the final step in the supply chain, bringing products from a distribution center to the consumer's location. This phase can be costly and challenging, particularly in urban areas with heavy traffic and high population density. Many companies in the F&B sector are exploring innovative solutions, such as micro-fulfillment centers, electric vehicles, and delivery drones, to enhance last-mile efficiency. E-commerce and food delivery services have intensified the demand for fast, reliable last-mile delivery, pushing companies to adopt flexible logistics strategies to meet consumer expectations.

Distribution Models (Direct-to-Retailer vs. Distribution Centers): Distribution strategies vary depending on the type of products, customer base, and business goals. Many large F&B companies operate through centralized distribution centers that allow for bulk storage and efficient dispatch to various retailers. Alternatively, some businesses choose direct-to-retailer distribution, which can reduce handling time and costs for high-demand items. With the rise of e-commerce and direct-to-consumer models, some F&B brands are establishing online sales channels, bypassing traditional retail channels altogether and shipping products directly to consumers.

Transportation Optimization: Given the high costs associated with transportation, F&B companies often employ strategies to optimize routes, reduce empty miles, and maximize vehicle capacity. This can involve route planning software, optimizing fleet management, and leveraging third-party logistics providers (3PLs) to improve efficiency. The use of data analytics is increasingly common to optimize delivery schedules and forecast demand, ensuring that distribution resources are used effectively.

3. Inventory Management and Procurement

Inventory management and procurement are essential to ensure F&B businesses maintain the right balance of stock to meet customer demand without excessive waste or storage costs. The unique characteristics of food products, particularly perishables, add a layer of complexity to inventory management.

Just-In-Time (JIT) Inventory: Just-In-Time (JIT) inventory management minimizes storage costs and reduces waste by aligning inventory closely with demand. F&B companies can order ingredients and materials as needed, thus minimizing the risk of spoilage for perishable items. However, JIT requires highly accurate demand forecasting and reliable supplier relationships, as any disruption in supply can lead to stockouts and missed sales.

Demand Forecasting: Accurate demand forecasting is critical for effective inventory management. F&B companies use historical data, seasonal trends, and advanced predictive analytics to forecast demand and plan inventory levels accordingly. For example, a restaurant chain may anticipate higher demand for ice cream in summer months or increased sales of seasonal products during holidays. Demand forecasting enables companies to make data-driven decisions, ensuring they have sufficient stock while minimizing waste.

Safety Stock and Buffer Inventory: Due to the unpredictable nature of demand and supply chain disruptions, many F&B companies maintain safety stock or buffer inventory. Safety stock serves as a contingency to accommodate unforeseen spikes in demand or delays in supply, particularly for high-demand products or critical ingredients. Balancing safety stock is crucial—too much can lead to waste and high holding costs, while too little increases the risk of stockouts.

Inventory Management Systems: Many F&B companies invest in inventory management software to streamline procurement and inventory tracking. These systems offer real-time visibility into stock levels, automate reorder processes, and provide analytics for informed decision-making. Some inventory systems are integrated with point-of-sale (POS) systems, enabling seamless tracking from purchase to consumption. Inventory management software can help reduce manual errors, improve efficiency, and allow managers to focus on more strategic tasks.

Supplier Relationship Management (SRM): Building strong relationships with suppliers is crucial for effective procurement. F&B companies need reliable suppliers to ensure consistent quality, timely delivery, and adherence to safety standards. Supplier relationship management (SRM) involves regularly communicating with suppliers, establishing performance benchmarks, and collaborating on ways to improve quality and reduce costs. Additionally, companies may engage in strategic sourcing, selecting suppliers based on their ability to offer competitive pricing, innovation, and sustainability initiatives.

The F&B supply chain is a complex network that requires careful management of sourcing, logistics, distribution, inventory, and procurement. Each component plays a vital role in ensuring that ingredients and finished products reach consumers in optimal condition. The global nature of the F&B industry, combined with the demand for fresh, high-quality ingredients, requires innovative supply chain strategies, including sustainable sourcing, cold chain logistics, and advanced inventory management techniques.

With the constant evolution of consumer preferences, technology, and regulatory standards, F&B companies must continuously adapt their supply chain practices to stay competitive. By focusing on efficiency, transparency, and collaboration, businesses in the F&B sector can build resilient supply chains that not only meet consumer needs but also contribute to the industry's sustainability and growth.

Chapter 5: Food Safety and Quality Standards

Food safety and quality standards are essential pillars of the Food and Beverage (F&B) industry. These standards ensure that food products are safe for consumption and meet the expectations of consumers in terms of taste, texture, and nutritional value. Food safety regulations are strictly enforced worldwide due to the potential risks associated with unsafe food, including foodborne illnesses and contamination. In this chapter, we will discuss the importance of food safety regulations, key quality control processes in the F&B industry, and widely recognized food safety certifications, such as HACCP and ISO.

1. Importance of Food Safety Regulations

Food safety regulations play a critical role in protecting public health by minimizing the risks associated with foodborne illnesses, contamination, and unsafe handling practices. These regulations provide a standardized framework that F&B companies must follow to ensure food products are safe, sanitary, and produced in controlled environments.

Protecting Public Health: Foodborne illnesses affect millions of people globally each year and can have serious health consequences. Common foodborne pathogens, such as Salmonella, E. coli, and Listeria, can lead to severe illness or even death if consumed. Regulatory bodies, such as the Food and Drug Administration (FDA) in the United States and the European Food Safety Authority (EFSA) in the EU, establish safety guidelines to reduce the incidence of such illnesses. Regulations cover areas such as sanitation, temperature control, and food handling practices, which are critical in preventing contamination throughout the supply chain.

Ensuring Consumer Confidence: Consistent food safety practices build consumer trust, as they assure customers that the products they consume meet stringent standards. A single food safety incident can severely damage a brand's reputation, leading to decreased consumer confidence, loss of sales, and potential legal action. By adhering to food safety regulations, F&B companies protect their brands and establish themselves as reliable, responsible producers.

Global Trade Compliance: Food safety regulations also play a crucial role in facilitating international trade. Many countries require imported food products to meet specific safety standards, which necessitates compliance from F&B companies that wish to export their products. Food safety standards, such as those set by the World Health Organization (WHO) and the Codex Alimentarius, serve as international benchmarks that help harmonize food safety practices across borders, promoting smoother trade and reducing barriers.

2. Quality Control Processes

Quality control in the F&B industry involves a series of procedures and tests aimed at ensuring that products meet specified standards for taste, appearance, safety, and nutritional content. Effective quality control processes are essential for maintaining product consistency, minimizing waste, and preventing contamination.

Standard Operating Procedures (SOPs): SOPs provide step-by-step instructions for performing tasks in a consistent manner, which helps maintain quality and safety across all production stages. In the F&B industry, SOPs cover processes such as ingredient handling, equipment cleaning, cooking temperatures, and packaging. By ensuring that all employees follow these protocols, companies can reduce the risk of human error, contamination, and product inconsistencies.

Quality Assurance Testing: Quality assurance testing involves examining samples of raw materials, in-process products, and finished goods to ensure they meet pre-defined quality standards. Tests may include sensory evaluations (taste, smell, appearance), chemical analysis (pH levels, fat content, preservatives), and microbiological testing to detect potential contaminants. Quality assurance testing provides real-time insights into product quality and enables early identification of issues, allowing companies to address them before the products reach consumers.

Hazard Analysis and Critical Control Points (HACCP): HACCP is a systematic approach to identifying, evaluating, and controlling potential hazards at each stage of the food production process. Originally developed by NASA, HACCP has become a fundamental tool in the F&B industry for preventing contamination and ensuring food safety. The process involves seven principles: hazard analysis, identifying critical control points (CCPs), establishing critical limits, monitoring procedures, corrective actions, verification, and record-keeping. By implementing HACCP, companies can systematically identify and manage risks, ensuring that critical safety standards are met.

Traceability and Recall Procedures: Traceability systems enable companies to track products from production through to distribution, which is crucial for managing product recalls if safety issues arise. In the event of contamination or a quality breach, traceability systems allow companies to quickly identify affected products and remove them from circulation, thereby protecting consumers. Many F&B companies use barcodes, RFID tags, and digital tracking systems to improve traceability, which enhances their ability to respond to quality incidents promptly.

3. Food Safety Certifications

Food safety certifications are formal recognition that an F&B company has met specific safety and quality standards. Certifications such as HACCP and ISO are globally recognized and reassure consumers and regulatory bodies that the company adheres to strict safety and quality practices. Certification can also provide a competitive advantage, as certified companies are perceived as more credible and trustworthy.

HACCP (Hazard Analysis and Critical Control Points): HACCP is one of the most widely recognized food safety certifications in the F&B industry. It focuses on identifying and controlling potential hazards at every step of the production process. HACCP certification is essential for many companies that want to export food products to other countries, as it demonstrates adherence to rigorous safety standards. To obtain HACCP certification, companies must develop and implement a HACCP plan, undergo regular audits, and provide thorough documentation to prove compliance.

ISO 22000: ISO 22000 is an internationally recognized food safety management system standard that integrates the principles of HACCP with ISO's risk management framework. ISO 22000 certification encompasses all stages of the food supply chain, from raw material production to food preparation and distribution. It includes guidelines on risk analysis, resource management, product realization, and continual improvement. By achieving ISO 22000 certification, F&B companies demonstrate their commitment to food safety and their ability to identify and mitigate risks effectively.

BRCGS (British Retail Consortium Global Standards): The BRCGS certification is widely accepted in the global food industry and is particularly common among companies that supply products to retailers. It covers food safety, quality, and legality, with a strong focus on risk management and continuous improvement. The BRCGS standard requires companies to establish documented quality management systems, comply with rigorous hygiene practices, and implement HACCP-based safety controls. BRCGS certification is beneficial for companies looking to supply large retailers and gain access to new markets.

SQF (Safe Quality Food): The SQF program is a food safety and quality certification recognized by the Global Food Safety Initiative (GFSI). It offers two levels of certification—Level 2 (food safety) and Level 3 (food safety and quality)—allowing companies to choose the level that best suits their needs. SQF certification is commonly sought by companies that supply products to North American retailers and want to demonstrate their commitment to safety and quality. The certification process involves detailed audits, training, and documentation of safety practices.

FSSC 22000 (Food Safety System Certification): FSSC 22000 is another GFSI-recognized certification, designed for companies involved in food production, packaging, and logistics. It combines ISO 22000 standards with additional requirements to meet GFSI benchmarks, covering areas such as allergen control, food fraud prevention, and hazard management. FSSC 22000 is particularly popular among companies that operate in multiple countries, as it demonstrates compliance with international food safety standards.

Food safety and quality standards are indispensable for ensuring that food products meet the highest levels of safety, consistency, and reliability. Regulatory requirements, quality control processes, and certifications all work together to protect consumers, maintain brand reputation, and facilitate trade across international markets. Through rigorous adherence to food safety standards and certifications like HACCP, ISO 22000, and BRCGS, F&B companies can build strong consumer trust, reduce the risk of foodborne illnesses, and differentiate themselves in a competitive market.

As the F&B industry continues to evolve, advancements in technology and increased consumer awareness are likely to drive even stricter safety standards. Companies must stay informed and adaptive, ensuring that their food safety and quality practices evolve alongside regulatory changes, emerging risks, and consumer expectations.

Chapter 6: Menu Planning and Development

Menu planning and development are essential components of any food and beverage (F&B) business. A well-crafted menu not only meets customer expectations but also aligns with the establishment's brand identity, operating costs, and revenue goals. This chapter explores the elements of creating a balanced menu, analyzing customer preferences and dietary trends, and employing effective menu costing and pricing strategies to achieve financial success.

1. Creating a Balanced Menu

A balanced menu is the backbone of any successful F&B operation. It should reflect a harmonious blend of flavors, textures, colors, and nutritional values while also supporting the establishment's culinary theme and customer expectations.

Variety and Diversity: A well-balanced menu provides a range of options to cater to different tastes and dietary needs. Offering diverse appetizers, main courses, sides, and desserts can appeal to a broad customer base and encourage repeat visits. Including a mix of vegetarian, vegan, gluten-free, and meat-based dishes ensures that customers with various dietary preferences and restrictions have options.

Seasonal and Fresh Ingredients: Incorporating seasonal and fresh ingredients not only enhances the menu's appeal but also reduces costs. Seasonal ingredients are generally more abundant, affordable, and flavorful, which contributes to a better customer experience. Fresh ingredients can also enhance the nutritional quality of dishes and provide customers with an authentic taste.

Flavor Balance and Texture: A successful menu includes a range of flavors (salty, sweet, sour, bitter, umami) and textures (crispy, creamy, chewy, tender) to create a dynamic dining experience. Balancing these elements ensures that each dish feels distinct and complementary to the rest of the menu, enhancing customer satisfaction and encouraging them to try multiple items.

Nutritional Balance: Health-conscious customers are increasingly interested in the nutritional profile of the food they consume. A balanced menu should include healthy options that provide a good mix of protein, fiber, and essential vitamins and minerals. Offering healthier dishes—such as salads, whole grains, and low-calorie options—can appeal to a wider audience without compromising on flavor.

Alignment with Brand Identity: The menu should reflect the unique identity and style of the establishment. For example, a fine dining restaurant might focus on gourmet dishes with premium ingredients, while a casual café could offer comfort food with a homestyle feel. Ensuring consistency in the menu helps strengthen the brand and creates a memorable experience for customers.

2. Analyzing Customer Preferences and Dietary Trends

Understanding customer preferences and dietary trends is key to menu success. By staying informed about current food trends and customer expectations, an F&B business can create a menu that resonates with its audience and remains relevant.

Customer Surveys and Feedback: Gathering direct feedback through surveys, comment cards, and online reviews can provide valuable insights into what customers enjoy and what they would like to see improved. Regularly analyzing feedback can help identify popular dishes, as well as any adjustments needed to enhance the menu.

Market Research and Competitor Analysis: Observing what competitors offer and studying market trends can reveal insights into popular items, pricing strategies, and customer demands. Analyzing local dining trends, such as the popularity of certain cuisines or dietary options, can help an F&B establishment stay competitive.

Dietary Trends and Health Considerations: As dietary awareness grows, more customers seek menu options that accommodate specific dietary needs, such as gluten-free, dairy-free, vegan, keto, and low-sodium diets. Recognizing these trends allows an F&B business to adapt its menu to meet demand and improve customer satisfaction.

Cultural and Regional Preferences: Understanding local tastes and cultural preferences can enhance menu appeal. In areas with diverse populations, offering multicultural dishes can attract a broader audience. Regional preferences also play a role, as certain ingredients or flavor profiles may be more popular in specific locations.

Use of Technology for Data-Driven Decisions: Technology can help F&B businesses analyze data related to sales patterns, customer demographics, and peak dining times. Many modern POS systems and CRM platforms provide data analytics that allows for informed decisions based on customer purchasing behavior. This data can reveal which dishes are most popular, helping businesses to refine their menus and optimize inventory.

3. Menu Costing and Pricing Strategies

Pricing a menu effectively is crucial for ensuring profitability while maintaining customer satisfaction. Menu costing and pricing strategies require careful calculation to balance food costs, operating expenses, and desired profit margins.

Ingredient Costing and Food Cost Percentage: Accurate ingredient costing is essential for setting prices that cover expenses and yield a profit. This involves determining the cost of each ingredient in a dish and calculating the total dish cost. Food cost percentage, which is the ratio of the cost of ingredients to the selling price, helps determine appropriate pricing. Typically, F&B businesses aim for a food cost percentage between 25% and 35%.

Overhead and Labor Costs: In addition to food costs, menu pricing should account for overhead expenses such as rent, utilities, and labor. Calculating these costs and factoring them into menu prices ensures that all expenses are covered. Labor-intensive dishes may require higher prices to account for the time and effort involved in preparation.

Menu Engineering and Contribution Margin: Menu engineering involves analyzing each menu item's popularity and profitability to optimize pricing and presentation. The contribution margin, or the difference between the selling price and the food cost, indicates the profitability of each item. By classifying menu items as stars (high profitability, high popularity), plow horses (low profitability, high popularity), puzzles (high profitability, low popularity), and dogs (low profitability, low popularity), F&B businesses can make strategic decisions about which items to promote or adjust.

Psychological Pricing Tactics: Using psychological pricing techniques can influence customers' perceptions of value. For instance, pricing items just below whole numbers (e.g., $9.99 instead of $10) can make prices seem more attractive. Anchoring high-value items at the top of a menu or including premium options alongside standard offerings can guide customer choices and encourage higher spending.

Balancing Value and Quality: Customers seek a balance between the price they pay and the quality they receive. Ensuring that menu items offer good value for money by maintaining quality ingredients and generous portions can foster customer loyalty. Additionally, creating a mix of price points within the menu allows customers to choose items that fit their budget.

Dynamic Pricing and Promotions: Dynamic pricing, which adjusts prices based on demand or seasonality, can help manage costs and maximize revenue. Promotions and special offers can attract customers during off-peak hours, helping to boost sales. Limited-time discounts, happy hours, and combo deals are popular strategies for driving traffic and increasing average ticket size.

Menu planning and development are fundamental to the success of any food and beverage business. A thoughtfully designed menu reflects the establishment's brand identity, appeals to customer preferences, and supports financial goals. By creating a balanced menu that incorporates diverse flavors and dietary options, analyzing market trends and customer preferences, and implementing effective costing and pricing strategies, F&B businesses can enhance customer satisfaction and profitability. With an adaptable approach to menu planning, an F&B establishment can meet the evolving demands of consumers and remain competitive in a dynamic industry.

Chapter 7: Kitchen Operations and Equipment

In the Food and Beverage (F&B) industry, kitchen operations are the backbone of any successful food service business, whether it's a fine dining restaurant, a casual café, or a large-scale catering operation. A well-organized kitchen equipped with the right technology and efficient workflow processes can greatly enhance productivity, food quality, and safety. In this chapter, we'll explore essential kitchen equipment and technologies, food preparation and cooking processes, and best practices for managing kitchen workflow and efficiency.

1. Key Kitchen Equipment and Technologies

Modern kitchens are equipped with a variety of specialized tools and technologies designed to facilitate food preparation, cooking, and storage. The choice of equipment depends on the type of food service operation and its specific needs, but certain tools are fundamental in nearly every kitchen.

Cooking Equipment:

Ovens: Commercial kitchens use various types of ovens, such as convection ovens (which use fans to circulate hot air for even cooking), combi-ovens (which combine steam and convection for versatile cooking), and pizza ovens. Each oven type serves specific cooking needs, from baking pastries to roasting meats.

Ranges and Stoves: A staple in most kitchens, stoves are used for tasks like sautéing, frying, and boiling. Gas stoves provide instant heat control, while electric and induction stoves offer consistent temperatures and energy efficiency.

Grills and Griddles: Grills impart a unique charred flavor to foods and are commonly used in restaurants that serve meats and grilled vegetables. Griddles provide a flat, even surface for cooking foods like pancakes, eggs, and burgers.

Deep Fryers: Essential in fast-food and casual dining establishments, deep fryers are used for foods that need to be cooked quickly at high temperatures, such as fries, chicken, and seafood.

Preparation Equipment:

Mixers: Heavy-duty mixers are used for tasks like dough preparation, mixing batters, and blending ingredients. Stand mixers with attachments for kneading, whisking, and chopping are particularly useful for bakeries and pizzerias.

Food Processors: These machines handle chopping, slicing, grating, and pureeing with speed and efficiency. They are particularly valuable for high-volume kitchens needing to process large quantities of ingredients.

Blenders: Blenders are indispensable for creating sauces, smoothies, soups, and purees. High-powered commercial blenders can handle tougher ingredients like ice, nuts, and fibrous vegetables.

Cutting and Slicing Machines: Slicers, peelers, and choppers help reduce the manual labor involved in food preparation. Meat slicers are common in delis and sandwich shops, while vegetable cutters increase speed and uniformity in food preparation.

Refrigeration and Storage:

Walk-in Coolers and Freezers: Large, high-capacity coolers and freezers are essential for storing perishable ingredients safely and efficiently in commercial kitchens. They help preserve the freshness of bulk ingredients, reducing waste and supporting menu consistency.

Blast Chillers: Often found in large-scale kitchens, blast chillers are used to rapidly cool cooked foods, helping to prevent bacterial growth and extend shelf life. This technology is essential for safe food storage and compliance with health regulations.

Dry Storage Units: Shelving, bins, and cabinets for dry goods are important in organizing non-perishable items, such as grains, canned foods, and spices, allowing for easy access and inventory control.

Cleaning and Sanitation:

Dishwashers and Glasswashers: Commercial-grade dishwashers can handle large volumes of dishes quickly, ensuring sanitation standards are met. Some kitchens also use specialized glasswashers for delicate items like wine glasses.

Hand Washing Stations: These are strategically placed to encourage staff to wash their hands frequently, which is essential in preventing contamination. Many stations include touchless faucets and soap dispensers for added sanitation.

Sanitizing Equipment: To prevent cross-contamination, kitchens often use sanitizing sprays, wipes, and UV sterilizers for knives, cutting boards, and other utensils. Food-safe sanitizers are especially important in areas where raw meats and vegetables are prepared.

2. Food Preparation and Cooking Processes

In a commercial kitchen, food preparation and cooking processes must be precise, consistent, and efficient. This involves planning, skilled techniques, and maintaining high standards in every step, from ingredient prep to plating.

Mise en Place: "Mise en place," a French culinary term meaning "putting in place," refers to the practice of organizing ingredients and tools before cooking begins. This includes tasks like chopping vegetables, portioning meats, and setting up spices and seasonings. Proper mise en place enables cooks to work more quickly and reduces errors, allowing for smoother service during busy periods.

Batch Cooking: For high-volume kitchens, batch cooking is a common technique where large quantities of food are prepared and cooked in advance, often in separate stages. For example, sauces and soups might be prepared in large batches and then portioned out as needed. Batch cooking helps streamline service and reduces the time needed to prepare each order individually.

Cooking Techniques:

Sautéing and Stir-frying: Quick, high-heat methods used for cooking small pieces of food, like vegetables, meats, or seafood. These techniques preserve the color, texture, and nutrients of the ingredients.

Roasting and Baking: Roasting involves cooking food at high temperatures to develop a caramelized exterior, while baking is a gentler method suited for breads, pastries, and casseroles.

Simmering and Boiling: These methods are used for foods that need to be softened or cooked thoroughly, such as pasta, grains, and stews.

Grilling and Broiling: Both methods involve cooking with direct heat, which imparts a smoky flavor and creates a crisp exterior. Broiling uses heat from above, while grilling uses heat from below.

Blanching and Shocking: Blanching involves briefly boiling vegetables, then plunging them into ice water to halt the cooking process. This method retains color and texture, and is commonly used in salad and vegetable prep.

3. Managing Kitchen Workflow and Efficiency

Efficient kitchen workflow is essential to meeting customer demands, especially during peak times. A well-organized kitchen with defined work zones, effective communication, and streamlined processes helps reduce wait times, prevent errors, and improve overall quality.

Kitchen Layout and Zoning: A commercial kitchen layout is often designed with specific zones for different tasks, such as preparation, cooking, plating, and cleaning. Each zone should have the equipment, tools, and supplies needed for its specific function. By strategically separating tasks, kitchens can reduce traffic, minimize the risk of cross-contamination, and create a smooth flow for staff as they move through each stage of meal preparation.

Workflow Optimization: To maximize efficiency, kitchen managers often establish standardized workflows based on the kitchen's layout and menu requirements. These workflows determine the sequence in which tasks are performed, allowing for seamless transitions between food prep, cooking, and plating. Tools like checklists, timers, and preparation guides can support staff in following these workflows, ensuring consistency and accuracy.

Team Roles and Responsibilities: In a commercial kitchen, each team member typically has a designated role, such as chef, sous chef, line cook, or dishwasher. Clear roles help prevent redundancy, improve accountability, and ensure each part of the process is managed by someone with the necessary expertise. Effective teamwork and communication, including the use of verbal cues and hand signals, help prevent bottlenecks and reduce confusion.

Lean Kitchen Principles: Adopting lean principles in kitchen operations can minimize waste, reduce clutter, and improve efficiency. This includes strategies like minimizing food waste, organizing tools and ingredients by frequency of use, and simplifying tasks. Lean principles also encourage staff to regularly assess workflows and make incremental improvements, which can lead to greater productivity and reduced operational costs over time.

Technology and Automation: Many modern kitchens incorporate technology to enhance workflow and increase speed. For instance, inventory management software helps track ingredient levels and automatically places orders when stocks are low, preventing shortages.

Automated cooking and preparation equipment, like conveyor belt ovens and food processors, reduce the manual labor required, freeing up staff to focus on more intricate tasks.

Effective kitchen operations rely on a combination of the right equipment, well-honed preparation and cooking processes, and a streamlined workflow. By investing in advanced technology and optimizing workflows, F&B businesses can increase efficiency, improve product quality, and enhance customer satisfaction. With clear roles, lean practices, and the latest equipment, commercial kitchens can meet the demands of a dynamic industry while maintaining safety, consistency, and high standards. As the industry evolves, continuous improvement in kitchen operations will remain essential for delivering quality food efficiently and profitably.

Chapter 8: Beverage Operations and Management

The beverage segment plays a significant role in the food and beverage (F&B) industry, offering a diverse range of products that appeal to various consumer preferences. Beverage operations span from the management of bars and cafés to the creation of sophisticated drink menus and the art of mixology. This chapter provides an in-depth exploration of different types of beverages, effective beverage menu design, and the nuances of managing bar operations.

1. Types of Beverages

Beverages can be broadly categorized into two main groups: alcoholic and non-alcoholic. Each category includes a vast variety of drinks, with their own unique production processes, flavors, and service requirements. Understanding the distinctions and specialties within each category is essential for any successful beverage operation.

Alcoholic Beverages: Alcoholic drinks are a staple of many restaurants, bars, and hospitality settings. They are created through fermentation or distillation processes and can range in alcohol content, flavor profile, and presentation.

Beer: One of the oldest and most popular alcoholic drinks, beer is typically made from grains (like barley), water, hops, and yeast. The beer industry has expanded with the craft beer movement, which focuses on unique flavors, local ingredients, and artisanal brewing methods. Beers are classified into categories such as lagers, ales, stouts, and pilsners, each with distinct characteristics.

Wine: Wine is made by fermenting grapes and other fruits, and it's often categorized by region, grape variety, and production method. The wine industry is diverse, including red, white, rosé, sparkling, and dessert wines, each of which is paired with specific foods to enhance flavor profiles. Wine education is crucial for staff, as wine pairing and proper serving techniques are essential for customer satisfaction.

Spirits: Spirits are distilled alcoholic beverages with a high alcohol content and include options like vodka, whiskey, gin, rum, and tequila. These drinks serve as a base for numerous cocktails and are also enjoyed neat or on the rocks. Each spirit has unique serving and storage guidelines, which bartenders should understand to ensure the best experience for patrons.

Cocktails and Mixed Drinks: Cocktails involve blending different types of alcohol, mixers, and flavoring agents. The art of mixology, which emphasizes balancing flavors and creating innovative drinks, is central to high-quality bar service. Classic cocktails like martinis, mojitos, and margaritas remain popular, while mixologists continue to create new recipes that incorporate seasonal ingredients and modern techniques.

Non-Alcoholic Beverages: Non-alcoholic drinks appeal to a broader audience, including those who don't consume alcohol or prefer healthier, caffeine-free, or low-sugar options. Non-alcoholic beverage menus have grown significantly, with an increased focus on health-conscious ingredients and artisanal preparation methods.

Soft Drinks and Sodas: Carbonated beverages, including colas, root beers, and fruit-flavored sodas, are a common choice for casual dining and quick-service restaurants. Some bars also offer house-made sodas or mocktails, blending creativity with traditional non-alcoholic options.

Coffee and Tea: Coffee and tea are globally popular beverages served in various forms, including espresso, cappuccino, chai, and matcha.

Specialty coffee shops focus on high-quality beans, brewing methods, and latte art, while tea houses offer diverse tea selections, from black and green teas to herbal infusions. Knowledge of brewing techniques, flavors, and origins is essential for establishments specializing in these drinks.

Juices and Smoothies: Fresh fruit and vegetable juices, as well as smoothies, appeal to health-conscious consumers. Cold-pressed juices and superfood smoothies are particularly popular in health-focused cafés and juice bars. High-quality juicing equipment and fresh ingredients are essential to maintain flavor and nutritional value.

Mocktails: Non-alcoholic cocktails, or mocktails, are crafted with the same care as alcoholic cocktails, often using syrups, fresh fruits, herbs, and exotic flavorings. Mocktails offer a sophisticated alternative to alcohol, allowing patrons to enjoy creative, refreshing beverages without the effects of alcohol.

2. Beverage Menu Design

A well-designed beverage menu can enhance the dining experience, increase sales, and reflect the unique personality of a restaurant or bar. The design process requires thoughtful consideration of audience preferences, pricing, ingredient selection, and presentation.

Understanding Audience Preferences: A successful beverage menu should be tailored to the establishment's target demographic. For instance, a high-end restaurant may offer an extensive wine list with premium wines, while a café might focus on specialty coffee drinks and artisanal teas. Studying customer preferences, local trends, and seasonal demands helps in creating a beverage menu that resonates with patrons.

Balancing the Menu: Beverage menus should provide a balanced selection across categories. Offering a mix of alcoholic and non-alcoholic options, classic and modern cocktails, and a range of price points allows customers to find something that suits their taste and budget. Additionally, highlighting specialty drinks, such as seasonal cocktails or limited-time offerings, keeps the menu fresh and interesting.

Pricing Strategy: Beverage pricing should align with the venue's overall pricing strategy. For alcoholic beverages, factors like alcohol content, brand reputation, and ingredient costs influence pricing. Non-alcoholic drinks like mocktails, house-made sodas, and specialty teas often carry higher margins, and offering them as add-ons can help boost revenue.

Menu Layout and Presentation: The layout of the beverage menu affects customer choices. Grouping beverages by category, including clear descriptions, and using enticing imagery can help guide customers. Creative names, brief ingredient lists, and visual elements that match the restaurant's ambiance add to the overall appeal. Many establishments also highlight signature drinks to showcase the unique offerings that set them apart from competitors.

Pairing Suggestions: Providing pairing suggestions can enhance customer experience, especially in establishments with a comprehensive food and beverage menu. For example, suggesting a crisp white wine with seafood or a robust red with steak encourages guests to try new pairings, enhancing their dining experience and potentially increasing the average check size.

3. Mixology and Bar Operations

Mixology and bar operations are essential aspects of any venue that offers alcoholic beverages. Skilled bartenders and efficient bar management practices are key to creating memorable drinks and ensuring smooth operations in a high-pressure environment.

The Art of Mixology: Mixology is the craft of preparing and creating cocktails. It requires an understanding of flavor profiles, ingredient pairings, and drink presentation. A well-trained mixologist can create complex drinks by balancing spirits, mixers, and garnishes, resulting in cocktails that are both visually appealing and flavorful. Modern mixology trends emphasize seasonal ingredients, exotic spices, and unique infusions, allowing for a more experimental and artisanal approach to cocktails.

Bar Setup and Equipment: Efficient bar operations rely on a well-organized setup and high-quality equipment. A typical bar station includes essentials such as cocktail shakers, strainers, jiggers, muddlers, and bar spoons. A bar layout designed for speed and accessibility helps bartenders move efficiently, reducing wait times for customers. Additionally, refrigeration units, ice machines, and garnishing stations are critical for maintaining product quality and quick service.

Inventory Management: Effective inventory management in bar operations ensures a steady supply of ingredients without overstocking or waste. Bar managers typically conduct regular inventory checks to monitor stock levels and identify high-demand items. Inventory management software can also track usage patterns, helping managers make informed purchasing decisions and minimize waste.

Staff Training and Customer Service: Bartenders must possess a thorough knowledge of the menu, drink-making techniques, and responsible alcohol service practices. Regular training on the latest mixology trends, customer service skills, and safety standards is essential for creating a positive bar environment. Customer service is paramount, as bartenders often serve as the primary point of contact with patrons, influencing their overall experience.

Responsible Alcohol Service: Responsible service of alcohol is a critical aspect of bar operations, especially in locations with strict liquor regulations. Bartenders should be trained in identifying signs of intoxication and implementing responsible serving practices. Many establishments also limit the number of drinks served per guest and offer alternatives, such as non-alcoholic options or smaller serving sizes, to promote a safe and enjoyable experience for all patrons.

The beverage sector in the F&B industry requires a deep understanding of various drink categories, strategic menu design, and efficient bar management. Beverage operations are not only about serving drinks but also about creating memorable experiences through quality products and customer interaction. From curating a balanced beverage menu to implementing effective bar operations and mixology, each aspect contributes to the overall success of an F&B establishment. As trends in health-conscious and artisanal beverages continue to evolve, establishments that prioritize innovation, quality, and customer satisfaction in their beverage offerings will stand out in a competitive market.

Chapter 9: Food and Beverage Service Standards

Delivering high-quality service is a cornerstone of success in the food and beverage (F&B) industry. Service standards define the experience customers can expect and help ensure consistency, professionalism, and customer satisfaction. This chapter examines various service types, essential customer service skills, and training methods to prepare staff for delivering excellent service.

1. Service Types in Food and Beverage

The type of service offered by an establishment depends on its concept, target market, and operational structure. Each service type has unique characteristics that influence the customer experience, efficiency, and service flow.

Table Service: Table service is common in full-service restaurants, ranging from casual dining to fine dining. In this type, servers take orders directly at the table and bring food and beverages to guests. This form of service can vary in formality and complexity:

Fine Dining: This involves highly trained servers, a structured meal sequence, and careful attention to detail. Servers assist with menu recommendations, wine pairing, and may perform tableside preparations. Service is often discreet and formal, focusing on a personalized dining experience.

Casual Dining: Casual dining offers a relaxed atmosphere with attentive but less formal service. Servers interact with guests to provide a friendly experience, though they may serve multiple tables at once and manage larger volumes than fine dining servers.

Buffet Service: Buffet service allows guests to serve themselves from a variety of dishes displayed on tables or counters. Common in hotels, events, and some casual dining settings, this style provides a broad selection of foods, from appetizers to desserts. Buffet service appeals to customers who value choice, speed, and the ability to try multiple dishes. However, maintaining food quality, cleanliness, and refilling items regularly are key to an effective buffet service.

Counter Service: Counter service is a popular choice for fast-food restaurants, coffee shops, and grab-and-go outlets. Customers order and pay at the counter, then receive their food for takeout or to consume on-site. This type of service emphasizes speed and convenience, making it ideal for high-traffic locations. Efficiency, accuracy, and a streamlined ordering process are essential to counter service, as customers expect minimal wait times.

Family-Style or Shared Service: Family-style service involves placing large portions of food on the table for guests to share, allowing them to serve themselves. It creates a communal atmosphere and is common in casual dining or themed restaurants. This style encourages group interaction and can reduce the server's workload, but it requires clear communication to ensure customers understand the self-serve format.

Room Service: Room service is primarily found in hotels and resorts, offering guests the convenience of enjoying meals in their private rooms. This service requires promptness, attention to detail, and careful food packaging. Room service can be costly and labor-intensive, but it enhances the guest experience by providing a personalized and flexible dining option.

Specialty Service (e.g., tableside or gueridon): Specialty service is often seen in high-end establishments and involves unique, personalized presentations. Examples include tableside cooking, where chefs or servers prepare dishes like flambé desserts or Caesar salads in front of the guest. This service style adds an element of entertainment, making the dining experience memorable and engaging.

2. Customer Service Skills in Food and Beverage

Exceptional customer service is key to customer loyalty, positive reviews, and repeat business. Service staff play a critical role in shaping the guest experience, making it essential for them to be skilled in interpersonal and technical abilities.

Effective Communication: Communication skills are at the heart of customer service in F&B. Servers must listen to customer needs, answer questions about the menu, and communicate orders accurately to the kitchen. Clear, polite, and friendly communication ensures customers feel valued and understood, while clear communication with coworkers helps streamline service.

Attentiveness: Attentiveness involves closely observing guests to anticipate their needs without being intrusive. This can mean refilling water glasses, noticing when a plate needs clearing, or addressing customer concerns promptly. Attentiveness shows guests they are important, enhancing their experience and contributing to positive feedback.

Product Knowledge: Staff should be well-versed in the menu, including ingredients, preparation methods, and potential allergens. Knowledgeable servers can make recommendations, answer questions, and address dietary restrictions confidently. Product knowledge also applies to beverages, where staff should understand basic drink pairings and non-alcoholic options.

Problem-Solving Skills: In fast-paced F&B environments, problems can arise, such as a delayed order or incorrect item. Skilled servers are proactive and resourceful in resolving issues efficiently, turning a potential negative experience into a positive one. For example, offering a complimentary dessert or drink in response to a delay can help mitigate dissatisfaction.

Time Management: Servers often handle multiple tables, requiring effective time management to ensure all guests receive timely and attentive service. Prioritizing tasks, multitasking, and staying organized are crucial, especially during peak hours. Good time management reduces stress for staff and improves the customer experience.

Professionalism and Etiquette: F&B staff should maintain a professional appearance, treat customers respectfully, and follow proper dining etiquette, such as addressing guests politely, serving from the correct side, and clearing dishes discreetly. Professionalism builds trust, allowing customers to relax and enjoy their experience.

Adaptability and Resilience: The F&B industry can be unpredictable, with unexpected rushes or challenging guests. Staff need to be adaptable, handling changing situations calmly and positively. A resilient attitude helps prevent burnout, particularly in high-pressure environments.

3. Training Staff for Excellent Service

Training is fundamental to achieving high service standards. A structured training program can ensure staff understand expectations, are knowledgeable about the menu, and can handle customer interactions confidently.

Orientation and Onboarding: New hires should begin with an orientation that introduces them to the company's values, mission, and service standards. Onboarding can include shadowing experienced servers, observing different service types, and learning customer service basics. A well-designed onboarding process gives new staff a strong foundation for success.

Product and Menu Training: Product knowledge is essential for servers to offer informed recommendations and answer questions confidently. Training should include a detailed review of the menu items, preparation methods, and key ingredients. Staff can also participate in taste testing, giving them firsthand experience with the menu offerings.

Service Technique Training: Servers need specific training on service techniques, including proper ways to serve, clear dishes, and handle special service requests. Role-playing scenarios, where staff practice common interactions, can help build confidence. Technique training also encompasses specialized services, like tableside preparation or wine service, for staff in fine dining or specialty restaurants.

Customer Service and Communication Skills: Customer service training focuses on communication, empathy, and handling challenging situations. Staff should learn how to greet customers warmly, respond to complaints professionally, and create a positive guest experience. Training can include exercises to improve active listening, nonverbal communication, and tactful conflict resolution.

Health, Safety, and Hygiene Training: Maintaining health and safety standards is critical in the F&B industry. Staff must be trained in proper hygiene practices, food handling procedures, and emergency protocols. Hygiene training includes washing hands regularly, handling food safely, and using sanitization procedures. Understanding health and safety regulations helps prevent foodborne illnesses and ensures a clean, safe environment for guests.

Continuous Improvement and Feedback: Training should not be a one-time event. Continuous improvement programs, including regular feedback sessions, refresher courses, and performance reviews, keep staff updated on best practices. Customer feedback also serves as a valuable training tool, helping staff understand areas for improvement.

Cross-Training: Cross-training staff to handle multiple roles, such as hosting, bartending, or working the kitchen, can improve flexibility and efficiency. Cross-training allows staff to support each other during busy periods and fosters a stronger team environment.

Service standards are the backbone of customer satisfaction in the F&B industry. By offering well-defined service types, instilling essential customer service skills, and implementing comprehensive training, establishments can elevate their service quality. The ability to provide consistent, professional, and personable service sets high-performing F&B businesses apart from competitors. Through continuous improvement and dedication to customer satisfaction, F&B staff can create memorable experiences that encourage repeat visits and positive recommendations, making excellent service an invaluable asset to any F&B business.

Chapter 10: Staff Training and Development

In the food and beverage (F&B) industry, staff training and development are key drivers of service quality, operational efficiency, and employee satisfaction. Effective training programs help ensure that both kitchen and service staff have the skills, knowledge, and confidence to deliver high standards of food safety, preparation, and customer service. This chapter explores the importance of training programs for F&B staff, highlights skill development and certification pathways, and examines the role of team building and communication in fostering a positive work environment.

1. Training Programs for Kitchen and Service Staff

Well-designed training programs lay the foundation for success in the F&B industry. By investing in systematic and comprehensive training, establishments can enhance service consistency, improve customer satisfaction, and reduce employee turnover. Training programs should be tailored to the unique needs of kitchen and service staff, as each role requires distinct technical skills, knowledge, and approaches to customer interactions.

Kitchen Staff Training:

Kitchen staff training focuses on food preparation, safety, and operational efficiency. Programs should cover various techniques, equipment handling, menu items, and hygiene practices to ensure consistent quality and safety.

Food Preparation and Cooking Techniques: Training should cover foundational cooking methods, including grilling, frying, sautéing, and baking. Advanced techniques can be introduced based on the establishment's menu and specialty dishes. Regular training on recipe adherence ensures consistency and quality in every dish.

Safety and Hygiene Practices: Kitchen staff must be trained on proper hygiene practices, including handwashing, sanitizing surfaces, and preventing cross-contamination. Programs should emphasize local food safety regulations, the importance of maintaining clean workstations, and proper handling of perishable ingredients.

Inventory and Waste Management: Efficient inventory management helps control costs and reduce food waste. Training staff on stock rotation, labeling systems, and portion control ensures minimal waste while maintaining freshness. Staff can also be trained to identify signs of spoilage and handle leftovers responsibly.

Equipment Operation and Maintenance: Kitchen equipment can be complex and requires careful handling to avoid accidents. Training should include safe usage, cleaning protocols, and maintenance procedures for appliances such as ovens, grills, and mixers.

Service Staff Training:

Service staff training emphasizes customer service skills, menu knowledge, and operational procedures. Programs should cover interaction etiquette, food and beverage presentation, and the skills needed to create a pleasant dining experience.

Customer Service Skills: Interpersonal skills, such as active listening, friendliness, and empathy, are vital for service staff. Training programs can include role-playing exercises to help staff respond effectively to customer needs and complaints.

Menu Knowledge: Service staff should be knowledgeable about the menu, including dish ingredients, preparation styles, and allergens. This allows them to make informed recommendations and provide accurate answers to customer inquiries.

Order Management and POS Training: Using a point-of-sale (POS) system efficiently is essential for accurate order processing and quick service. Training should cover order entry, modifications, bill splitting, and handling payments to ensure accuracy and speed.

Health and Safety Protocols: Service staff should be trained on hygiene protocols, such as proper handwashing and handling of dishes and utensils. They should also know how to manage food allergies and dietary restrictions to ensure a safe dining experience.

2. Skill Development and Certifications

In addition to initial training, ongoing skill development and certifications can enhance staff competency, expand career opportunities, and ensure compliance with industry standards. Offering employees access to certification programs is a valuable investment that demonstrates a commitment to quality and professionalism.

Culinary Skills Development:

For kitchen staff, culinary training can range from basic cooking methods to advanced culinary arts. Programs may include:

Knife Skills: Proper knife techniques improve efficiency and safety in the kitchen. Training on knife handling, sharpening, and cutting techniques helps kitchen staff work more effectively and consistently.

Advanced Cooking Techniques: Specialized training on techniques such as sous-vide, fermentation, and molecular gastronomy can enhance the culinary offerings in high-end establishments. Such skills development allows for a more diverse and innovative menu.

Food Safety and Sanitation Certifications:

Food safety certifications, like HACCP (Hazard Analysis Critical Control Point) and ServSafe, are critical for F&B establishments to prevent foodborne illnesses and maintain compliance. Many regulatory bodies require these certifications, making them essential for professional kitchen staff.

HACCP Certification: This certification educates kitchen staff on identifying, evaluating, and controlling food safety hazards. It is particularly important for handling perishable goods and high-risk items like seafood and poultry.

ServSafe Certification: Widely recognized in the industry, ServSafe offers training in food handling, sanitation, and allergy management, making it a valuable credential for both kitchen and service staff.

Beverage Knowledge and Mixology Certifications:

For staff in beverage service, such as bartenders and sommeliers, certifications in mixology, wine knowledge, and responsible alcohol service are essential for delivering a high-quality experience.

Certified Mixologist: This certification provides comprehensive training in cocktail-making, spirits knowledge, and bar operations, enabling bartenders to create an engaging beverage experience for customers.

Sommelier Certification: Wine certifications, such as those offered by the Court of Master Sommeliers, can deepen beverage staff's knowledge of wine varieties, regions, and pairings, allowing them to enhance customer satisfaction with expert recommendations.

Customer Service and Management Certifications:

For those aiming to move into supervisory or management roles, customer service and hospitality management certifications are valuable. Programs from institutions like the American Hotel & Lodging Educational Institute (AHLEI) offer hospitality-focused training in leadership, conflict resolution, and team management.

3. Team Building and Communication

A strong, cohesive team is essential for creating a positive workplace environment and delivering exceptional customer service. Team building and effective communication not only improve collaboration but also help reduce stress and improve employee morale.

Building Teamwork in the Workplace:

Effective teamwork is essential for smooth operations in the F&B industry, where multiple departments must work together to serve customers effectively. Team-building activities can foster relationships, encourage trust, and enhance cooperation.

Regular Team Meetings: Scheduling regular team meetings allows staff to discuss challenges, share ideas, and celebrate achievements. Meetings can include open forums for feedback, allowing team members to feel heard and valued.

Team-Building Exercises: Activities like role-playing, problem-solving games, and cross-training can build trust and strengthen relationships. Team-building exercises encourage staff to support each other, communicate effectively, and work together to provide seamless service.

Recognizing and Celebrating Success: Recognizing employee achievements, such as meeting sales goals or receiving positive customer feedback, can boost morale and motivate staff. Celebrations and rewards for team accomplishments foster a sense of pride and encourage continuous improvement.

Effective Communication Practices:

Clear communication is critical for ensuring that kitchen and service staff work together effectively. Establishing strong communication channels helps prevent misunderstandings, reduces errors, and promotes a positive work culture.

Pre-Shift Meetings (Line-Up): Conducting a brief meeting before each shift can help align the team on daily priorities, special menu items, and anticipated challenges. It also serves as an opportunity for managers to update staff on any policy changes or promotions.

Clear Communication Protocols: Establishing clear protocols for order taking, food running, and kitchen coordination helps reduce confusion and minimize delays. Using simple, consistent terminology for specific actions or processes can also improve efficiency.

Encouraging Feedback and Open Dialogue: Creating a culture of open dialogue, where team members feel comfortable providing feedback, helps identify areas for improvement. Constructive feedback between the kitchen and front-of-house staff ensures that operations run smoothly, and any issues are promptly addressed.

Conflict Resolution and Stress Management:

In a high-pressure environment, conflicts or stressful situations can arise. Training staff on conflict resolution techniques helps maintain a positive atmosphere and avoid escalation.

Conflict Resolution Training: Training on active listening, empathy, and finding common ground can help employees resolve conflicts amicably. Encouraging staff to approach issues calmly and seek management assistance if needed promotes a respectful environment.

Stress Management Techniques: High-paced environments can lead to stress and burnout. Providing training on stress management, such as breathing exercises or short breaks, can help staff maintain their composure and focus during busy periods.

Investing in comprehensive staff training and development programs equips F&B businesses to maintain high standards, improve team morale, and boost productivity. Through targeted training for kitchen and service staff, continuous skill development, and fostering a culture of communication and teamwork, establishments can create a supportive environment that promotes personal growth and operational excellence. By prioritizing staff development, F&B businesses not only enhance customer satisfaction but also build a resilient workforce capable of adapting to the industry's demands.

Chapter 11: Health and Nutrition in Food and Beverage

With growing awareness of health and wellness, consumers increasingly prioritize nutritional value, dietary needs, and healthier menu options when dining out. This chapter explores the fundamentals of nutritional requirements, the importance of offering nutritious and healthy options, and strategies for catering to various dietary restrictions in the food and beverage (F&B) industry. By understanding these aspects, establishments can create menus that appeal to a broader audience, meet customer health needs, and align with modern dietary trends.

1. Understanding Nutritional Requirements

To effectively incorporate health-focused items on the menu, F&B businesses must first understand basic nutritional needs and how they impact health and wellness. Nutrition involves the intake of essential nutrients, including macronutrients (carbohydrates, proteins, and fats) and micronutrients (vitamins and minerals), that support bodily functions, energy production, and overall well-being.

Macronutrients and Energy Balance:

Carbohydrates: The primary source of energy, especially for high-activity levels. F&B businesses often focus on offering a mix of simple carbohydrates (found in fruits and sugars) and complex carbohydrates (from grains and legumes) to provide both quick and sustained energy.

Proteins: Essential for building and repairing tissues, proteins are vital for muscle growth, immune function, and hormone production. Common protein sources include meats, dairy, legumes, and plant-based proteins, allowing establishments to cater to diverse dietary preferences.

Fats: Though often avoided, fats are crucial for energy storage, brain health, and nutrient absorption. Offering healthier fat sources, like those from avocados, nuts, and olive oil, appeals to health-conscious customers while still providing essential fatty acids.

Micronutrients and Health Maintenance:

Micronutrients, such as vitamins and minerals, support various physiological functions. Calcium and vitamin D are essential for bone health, iron supports blood health, and antioxidants (e.g., vitamins C and E) help combat inflammation and aging. Offering a variety of fruits, vegetables, and nutrient-rich ingredients on the menu allows establishments to contribute positively to customers' health.

Dietary Fiber and Digestive Health:

Dietary fiber, found in whole grains, fruits, and vegetables, is crucial for digestive health, aiding in regularity and maintaining gut health. High-fiber foods are also known to promote satiety, making them an excellent choice for customers aiming to manage weight or blood sugar levels.

Understanding these nutritional components enables F&B businesses to create balanced dishes that align with customer health goals. By offering meals that provide the right macronutrient balance and are rich in essential vitamins and minerals, restaurants and food service providers can attract health-focused clientele and build a reputation for well-rounded meals.

2. Incorporating Healthy Options into the Menu

Offering nutritious and health-conscious options on the menu is a strategic way to meet customer demand for healthier dining choices. This involves designing dishes with balanced portions, using fresh ingredients, and embracing diverse culinary approaches to appeal to different dietary preferences.

Utilizing Fresh and Seasonal Ingredients:

Fresh ingredients not only offer superior taste but are also typically more nutrient-dense than processed foods. Incorporating seasonal fruits and vegetables helps establishments take advantage of peak freshness while also supporting local agriculture. Many customers also associate freshness with health, so this approach can improve menu appeal.

Reducing Processed and Refined Ingredients:

Processed foods often contain added sugars, unhealthy fats, and preservatives, which can detract from nutritional value. By reducing processed ingredients and opting for whole foods like grains, legumes, and lean proteins, F&B providers can enhance the nutritional profile of their menu. For instance, using whole-grain bread instead of refined flour, or natural sweeteners like honey and agave in place of sugar, are popular approaches.

Offering Balanced and Nutrient-Dense Meals:

Balanced dishes that incorporate a variety of nutrient-dense ingredients appeal to customers seeking a wholesome dining experience. For example, offering meals that combine lean proteins, vegetables, and whole grains can help meet daily nutritional needs without excessive calories or unhealthy fats.

Calorie-Conscious and Portion Control Options:

With many customers focusing on calorie management, providing lighter menu items or smaller portion sizes can cater to their preferences. This approach is especially effective in settings like fast-casual dining, where customers may want quick but nutritious options. Listing calorie information or marking healthier options on the menu also helps customers make informed choices.

Incorporating Superfoods and Health Trends:

Superfoods like kale, quinoa, chia seeds, and berries are popular choices among health-conscious consumers. These foods are rich in antioxidants, fiber, and essential nutrients, making them ideal for enhancing the nutritional value of dishes. Establishments can feature these ingredients in salads, smoothies, or main dishes to attract health-focused diners and tap into current dietary trends.

3. Addressing Dietary Restrictions

The F&B industry faces a growing need to cater to various dietary restrictions, whether due to allergies, lifestyle choices, or specific health conditions. By accommodating these needs, restaurants can improve customer satisfaction, build customer loyalty, and reach a broader audience.

Food Allergies and Intolerances:

Food allergies, such as those to peanuts, shellfish, and gluten, can pose significant health risks if not properly managed. Food intolerances, like lactose intolerance, can also cause discomfort. To cater to these needs:

Clear Ingredient Labels: Menus should clearly indicate allergenic ingredients or provide allergen menus that list potential allergens in each dish.

Cross-Contamination Prevention: Establishing protocols for preventing cross-contamination is crucial, especially in kitchens handling common allergens. Using separate preparation areas, utensils, and cooking surfaces helps avoid accidental exposure.

Vegan and Vegetarian Options:

The demand for vegan and vegetarian options is rising due to health, ethical, and environmental concerns. Incorporating plant-based dishes that replace animal products with vegetables, legumes, and plant-based proteins appeals to this demographic. Vegan dishes, which exclude all animal products, require creative substitutions like tofu, tempeh, and plant-based milk.

Plant-Based Alternatives: Innovative plant-based proteins, such as jackfruit for "pulled meat" dishes or chickpeas in salads, allow chefs to create satisfying meatless options. Offering versatile dishes that can be easily modified for vegan or vegetarian diets also enhances menu flexibility.

Gluten-Free Options:

Gluten intolerance and celiac disease necessitate the availability of gluten-free options. Using gluten-free grains like quinoa, rice, and buckwheat allows establishments to offer satisfying meals that cater to gluten-sensitive customers.

Gluten-Free Ingredients and Cooking Practices: Chefs must be cautious when preparing gluten-free items, as cross-contamination with gluten-containing ingredients can be problematic. Clear labeling, dedicated preparation areas, and alternative flours (such as almond or coconut flour) are key to offering safe, gluten-free dishes.

Low-Carb and Keto-Friendly Options:

Low-carb and ketogenic (keto) diets are popular among individuals focusing on weight loss or blood sugar management. These diets emphasize low carbohydrate intake while increasing fat and protein consumption. F&B providers can incorporate keto-friendly items, such as dishes with lean meats, avocados, and leafy greens, to attract customers following these dietary plans.

Dairy-Free and Lactose-Free Options:

For customers with lactose intolerance or a preference for dairy-free options, establishments can use plant-based milk (such as almond, oat, or soy milk) and dairy alternatives like coconut-based yogurts. These substitutions are widely used in cafes and restaurants offering coffee, smoothies, and desserts, making it easier for dairy-free diners to enjoy their experience.

Diabetic-Friendly and Low-Sugar Options:

For individuals managing diabetes, low-sugar and carbohydrate-controlled options are essential. Using natural sweeteners, like stevia or monk fruit, and offering dishes with balanced macronutrients allows F&B businesses to cater to diabetic customers. Reducing or eliminating added sugars in recipes is also a thoughtful approach for a broader health-conscious clientele.

Ethnic and Cultural Dietary Considerations:

Certain cultural or religious practices require dietary restrictions, such as halal, kosher, or Jain diets. Providing options that adhere to these requirements or offering the flexibility to customize dishes helps establishments connect with diverse cultural groups. Staff training on cultural dietary laws and preparation techniques ensures respectful and safe service.

In today's health-conscious and diverse society, the ability to offer nutritious, balanced, and accommodating menu options has become essential for F&B businesses. Understanding nutritional fundamentals, incorporating fresh and health-focused ingredients, and accommodating dietary restrictions can significantly enhance the dining experience and broaden the appeal of a restaurant or food service establishment. By making informed, inclusive menu choices, F&B businesses can meet evolving consumer expectations, promote health and wellness, and establish themselves as customer-centric and progressive dining destinations.

Chapter 12: Marketing and Branding for Food and Beverage Businesses

In the competitive landscape of the food and beverage (F&B) industry, effective marketing and branding are essential for creating a distinctive identity, attracting customers, and fostering loyalty. This chapter explores branding strategies specific to F&B businesses, the role of digital marketing and social media, and the importance of promotions, loyalty programs, and customer engagement. These elements, when well-integrated, allow F&B establishments to build meaningful connections with customers and maintain a strong market presence.

1. Branding Strategies for Food and Beverage Businesses

Branding in the F&B industry goes beyond a logo or color scheme; it encompasses the entire experience a business provides, from the quality of food and ambiance to the customer service. Strong branding helps distinguish a business in a crowded market, builds trust, and creates a lasting impression.

Establishing a Unique Brand Identity:

Brand identity is the foundation of how a business presents itself to the public. In the F&B sector, this includes the food style, interior design, service approach, and even the name and logo. Crafting a brand identity requires defining what makes the business unique, such as its commitment to sustainability, use of local ingredients, or a specific cuisine focus.

Mission and Vision: Clearly defining the brand's mission (why it exists) and vision (what it aims to achieve) can guide all aspects of business operations and ensure consistency in the brand's message. For example, an F&B business with a mission to offer "farm-to-table dining" will prioritize sourcing from local farms and highlighting freshness.

Brand Voice and Personality: A brand voice conveys the business's personality and values, whether it's casual and fun, upscale and refined, or family-friendly and welcoming. This voice should resonate across marketing channels, from social media posts to in-store signage, helping customers identify and relate to the brand.

Creating a Memorable Brand Experience:

In the F&B industry, customer experience is a critical component of branding. Memorable dining experiences encourage customers to return and recommend the establishment to others.

Atmosphere and Ambiance: The design, lighting, seating arrangements, and overall atmosphere should align with the brand identity. For example, a modern, minimalistic café brand may focus on clean lines and neutral colors, while a family-oriented restaurant might emphasize comfort with a cozy decor.

Consistent Quality: Consistency in food quality and service is essential for building a trustworthy brand. F&B establishments need to maintain high standards in every interaction, ensuring customers experience the same quality each time they visit.

Customer-Centric Approach: Focusing on customer preferences and feedback helps create an experience that customers value. Understanding what appeals to the target audience allows businesses to tailor their offerings, from menu design to service style.

2. Digital Marketing and Social Media

Digital marketing is a powerful tool for F&B businesses to reach a broad audience, engage with customers, and promote brand values. In recent years, social media platforms have become especially influential, as they allow direct communication with customers and provide a platform for brand storytelling.

Leveraging Social Media Platforms:

Each social media platform offers unique opportunities to reach customers. Platforms like Instagram and TikTok are visual-driven, making them ideal for F&B brands to showcase food photos, restaurant ambiance, and behind-the-scenes content. Facebook is useful for event announcements and engaging local communities, while Twitter can facilitate quick, real-time interactions with customers.

Visual Content: High-quality photos and videos are critical in the F&B industry, as visual appeal plays a significant role in attracting customers. Well-composed images of dishes, creatively styled drinks, and the restaurant environment can generate interest and encourage customers to visit.

Influencer Marketing: Collaborating with food bloggers, influencers, and social media personalities can extend a brand's reach to a broader audience. Influencers often have dedicated followers who trust their recommendations, and an endorsement can boost visibility and credibility.

User-Generated Content: Encouraging customers to share their dining experiences through hashtags or photo tags helps create a sense of community and authenticity. Reposting or featuring user-generated content on the business's social media page can reinforce a connection with customers and serve as valuable word-of-mouth marketing.

Content Marketing and Storytelling:

Content marketing allows F&B businesses to share their story, values, and expertise with customers. Telling the brand story — such as the inspiration behind the cuisine, the chef's journey, or sustainability efforts — builds an emotional connection and enhances brand authenticity.

Blogging and Recipes: Sharing recipes, food preparation tips, or articles about ingredients used in the restaurant can engage customers and establish the brand as a thought leader. This type of content can also improve search engine visibility and attract food enthusiasts to the brand's website.

Email Marketing: Building an email list allows businesses to keep customers informed about new menu items, special events, and exclusive promotions. Regular newsletters with personalized offers can enhance loyalty and encourage repeat visits.

Promotions and Offers on Digital Platforms: Limited-time offers, discounts, and seasonal promotions can generate excitement and boost sales. Offering exclusive digital coupons or special deals for followers can also increase social media engagement and encourage customer loyalty.

3. Promotions, Loyalty Programs, and Customer Engagement

Promotions and loyalty programs are essential tools for retaining customers and increasing the frequency of visits. Engaging with customers beyond the initial interaction helps strengthen relationships and turn one-time diners into repeat patrons.

Promotions and Special Offers:

Promotions, such as discounts, happy hours, or limited-time offers, attract customers by adding a sense of urgency. These campaigns can be seasonal, aligned with holidays, or even random "surprise" deals to encourage unplanned visits.

Holiday and Seasonal Promotions: Holiday-themed offers or special seasonal menus can capitalize on high-traffic periods. Limited-edition items or themed meals attract customers seeking unique experiences and create buzz around the brand.

Event-Based Marketing: Hosting events, like live music nights, wine tastings, or chef-led workshops, provides customers with reasons to visit beyond dining. These events can create memorable experiences that foster customer loyalty and encourage attendees to share their experiences on social media.

Loyalty Programs and Rewards:

Loyalty programs incentivize repeat visits by rewarding customers for their patronage. These programs not only retain customers but also gather valuable data on purchasing habits and preferences.

Point-Based Systems: Customers earn points for each purchase, which can later be redeemed for rewards like discounts or free items. Many point-based programs can be managed digitally through mobile apps, simplifying tracking and encouraging regular engagement.

Subscription and Membership Programs: Offering a subscription-based membership, where customers pay a monthly or yearly fee for exclusive discounts or VIP treatment, can attract loyal customers and provide a steady revenue stream.

Personalized Rewards: Personalizing rewards based on customers' preferences or purchasing history makes loyalty programs more appealing. For example, offering a free dessert on a customer's birthday or a special discount on their favorite dish adds a personal touch.

Engaging Customers through Feedback and Surveys:

Engaging customers for feedback after their dining experience helps businesses understand customer satisfaction levels and identify areas for improvement. Additionally, responding to online reviews or survey results shows customers that their opinions are valued.

Online Reviews and Ratings: Managing and responding to reviews on platforms like Google, Yelp, and TripAdvisor can influence prospective customers' decisions. Acknowledging positive feedback and professionally addressing negative reviews strengthens the brand's reputation.

Customer Surveys: Brief surveys after dining experiences provide valuable insights into customer satisfaction, menu preferences, and service quality. Survey responses can guide menu changes, service improvements, and even new offerings based on customer demand.

Marketing and branding are critical for F&B businesses aiming to attract customers and stand out in a competitive market. By developing a clear brand identity, leveraging digital platforms for marketing, and creating engaging promotions and loyalty programs, F&B businesses can establish strong connections with customers and build lasting loyalty. Effective branding strategies and proactive engagement foster a positive brand image, helping establishments thrive in an ever-evolving industry. In the modern F&B landscape, an integrated approach to marketing not only draws in new customers but also cultivates a community of loyal patrons who support the business over time.

Chapter 13: Financial Management in Food and Beverage

Financial management is a core component of success in the food and beverage (F&B) industry, where tight margins and fluctuating costs make strategic planning essential. This chapter provides an in-depth look at the financial aspects specific to F&B, including cost control and budgeting, profitability analysis, key financial ratios, and revenue management techniques. By mastering these elements, F&B managers and owners can maintain financial health, increase profitability, and make informed decisions that contribute to long-term success.

1. Cost Control and Budgeting

Cost control and budgeting form the foundation of financial management in any F&B business. Given the industry's narrow profit margins, efficient cost management is crucial for profitability.

Understanding Key Cost Components:

F&B businesses face a range of costs, but the primary categories include food costs, labor costs, and overhead expenses.

Food Costs: Food costs refer to the expenses associated with purchasing ingredients. Managing food costs effectively is critical, as fluctuations in ingredient prices can directly impact the bottom line. Effective procurement practices, seasonal purchasing, and menu engineering help control these costs.

Labor Costs: In addition to wages, labor costs include payroll taxes, benefits, and other compensation-related expenses. For many F&B businesses, labor costs make up a significant portion of expenses. Staffing optimization, training, and shift planning can help minimize unnecessary labor expenses without compromising service quality.

Overhead Costs: These include rent, utilities, insurance, and other fixed and variable costs not directly linked to food or labor. Overhead costs must be carefully monitored and budgeted to ensure they don't erode profits.

Developing and Managing a Budget:

A budget is a financial plan that allocates resources to achieve specific financial goals. In F&B, budgets often cover projected sales, direct costs, and operational expenses.

Creating Realistic Projections: To create an accurate budget, managers must understand historical sales data, market trends, and customer preferences. Projections based on past performance and anticipated changes (such as seasonal demand) help set realistic targets.

Tracking and Adjusting Costs: Once the budget is established, it's important to regularly track actual spending and compare it to budgeted figures. Any significant deviations should be analyzed to identify their cause, and adjustments should be made to keep the business financially aligned.

Forecasting for Variability: The F&B industry is subject to seasonal variations, special events, and trends. Managers should anticipate these changes by adjusting budgets and reallocating resources to ensure that high-demand periods are supported and low-demand periods are managed efficiently.

2. Profitability Analysis and Key Financial Ratios

Profitability analysis is essential for understanding how well a business is generating returns. Using key financial ratios allows managers to assess performance, compare it to industry benchmarks, and make informed decisions for improvement.

Gross Profit and Net Profit Analysis:

Gross Profit: Gross profit is calculated by subtracting the cost of goods sold (COGS) from total revenue. This figure shows the profitability of the core operations and reveals if food costs are under control.

Net Profit: Net profit, or the "bottom line," is calculated by subtracting all expenses, including operational and non-operational costs, from total revenue. This figure provides insight into overall profitability after all costs have been accounted for.

Key Financial Ratios in F&B:

Food Cost Percentage: Calculated as (Total Food Costs / Total Revenue) × 100, this ratio measures how much of revenue is consumed by food costs. A typical target for many F&B businesses is around 28-35%, though it varies by establishment type.

Labor Cost Percentage: Labor cost percentage is calculated as (Total Labor Costs / Total Revenue) × 100. This metric helps assess if labor expenses are in line with revenue. The labor cost target varies depending on service style, with full-service restaurants often budgeting around 25-35% and quick-service restaurants aiming lower.

Prime Cost Percentage: Prime costs include food and labor, which are often the largest expenses. The prime cost percentage, calculated as

(Food Cost + Labor Cost) / Total Revenue, is a key indicator of overall cost efficiency. For F&B establishments, keeping the prime cost below 60% is generally desirable.

Profit Margin Ratios: Profit margin ratios include gross profit margin and net profit margin. They are essential for understanding profitability relative to revenue. Gross profit margin is (Gross Profit / Total Revenue) × 100, and net profit margin is (Net Profit / Total Revenue) × 100. Higher margins indicate better cost control and profitability.

Inventory Turnover Ratio: This ratio, calculated as (Cost of Goods Sold / Average Inventory), measures how often inventory is sold and replenished. A higher turnover rate indicates efficient inventory management, while a low rate may signal overstocking or waste.

Return on Investment (ROI): ROI evaluates the profitability of investments by comparing the net profit generated to the amount invested. This is particularly important for capital-intensive F&B projects, such as new equipment or facility upgrades.

3. Revenue Management Techniques

Revenue management in F&B involves strategies to maximize revenue potential by adjusting pricing, optimizing menu offerings, and increasing table turnover.

Dynamic Pricing and Menu Engineering:

Pricing strategy directly impacts revenue generation. Dynamic pricing involves adjusting prices based on demand, seasonality, or other external factors. Menu engineering, on the other hand, focuses on optimizing menu items based on profitability and popularity.

Dynamic Pricing: Some F&B businesses, particularly those with high customer demand fluctuations (like bars or tourist restaurants), use dynamic pricing. For instance, prices may be higher during peak hours or on special occasions. Understanding customer behavior helps in implementing this approach effectively.

Menu Engineering: Menu engineering involves categorizing items based on profitability and popularity, often dividing them into four quadrants — stars (popular and profitable), puzzles (profitable but not popular), plowhorses (popular but less profitable), and dogs (neither popular nor profitable). This analysis helps managers make strategic menu adjustments, like promoting stars, reworking puzzles, or replacing dogs.

Table Turnover and Seating Optimization:

For restaurants, efficient table turnover is critical for maximizing revenue. This requires balancing quick service without rushing customers, optimizing table layout for different group sizes, and reducing wait times. Faster table turnover translates to more customers served per day, increasing total revenue.

Staff Efficiency and Training: Well-trained staff can improve service speed and customer satisfaction, enabling higher table turnover. Cross-training staff members to handle multiple tasks, such as greeting guests and serving, reduces waiting time and improves operational flow.

Reservation and Seating Management: Technology can help optimize seating and reservations, reducing waiting times and ensuring that tables are used effectively. Apps and systems that manage online reservations, walk-ins, and waitlists help minimize downtime and maximize occupancy.

Upselling and Cross-Selling:

Upselling and cross-selling are powerful strategies for increasing revenue per customer. Upselling involves encouraging customers to purchase a more expensive item (e.g., suggesting a premium wine), while cross-selling involves offering complementary items (e.g., a side dish or dessert).

Training Staff in Sales Techniques: Training staff to recommend items in a friendly, unobtrusive manner is key to successful upselling and cross-selling. Staff should be knowledgeable about menu options and understand how to suggest items that enhance the dining experience.

Creating Combo Deals and Add-Ons: Combo deals, such as a meal with a drink and dessert, encourage customers to spend more. Offering small add-ons, like sauces, toppings, or premium ingredients, allows customers to customize their meal and increases the check size.

Financial management in the F&B industry requires a comprehensive approach that includes cost control, budgeting, profitability analysis, and revenue optimization. Through effective budgeting, monitoring key financial ratios, and implementing revenue management strategies, F&B businesses can achieve financial stability and increase profitability. Financially sound businesses can reinvest in improving quality, expanding offerings, and attracting more customers, ultimately leading to sustained success in a highly competitive market.

Chapter 14: Food and Beverage Technology Trends

In the modern food and beverage (F&B) industry, technology has become integral to operations, transforming the ways businesses operate, serve customers, and make decisions. From digital ordering systems to data analytics and artificial intelligence, technology trends are reshaping the industry to be more efficient, customer-friendly, and adaptive. This chapter explores the critical roles technology plays, focusing on digital ordering and payment systems, the use of data analytics, and AI's influence in creating a smarter and more resilient F&B sector.

1. Role of Technology in Modern F&B Operations

Technology in F&B today is more than just an add-on; it's a foundational component that streamlines processes, enhances customer experiences, and improves operational efficiency.

Operational Efficiency:

Technology helps optimize daily operations, from inventory management to employee scheduling. Automation software assists with repetitive tasks, reducing the likelihood of errors and freeing up time for employees to focus on customer service. Additionally, technology aids in maintaining consistent quality by streamlining kitchen workflows and enabling better control over food preparation processes.

Customer Experience Enhancement:

The customer journey in F&B is becoming increasingly digital. Many restaurants now offer pre-ordering through apps, enabling customers to place their orders before arriving. This convenience reduces wait times, improves table turnover, and enhances overall customer satisfaction. Additionally, customer relationship management (CRM) systems allow businesses to remember customer preferences, enabling more personalized service and fostering loyalty.

Inventory and Waste Management:

Inventory control systems that use technology help F&B businesses keep accurate track of stock levels, forecast demand, and prevent over-ordering. By reducing waste and ensuring that ingredients are used efficiently, these systems save money and support sustainability goals.

Supply Chain Visibility:

Technologies such as blockchain and the Internet of Things (IoT) offer increased visibility into the F&B supply chain. Blockchain can provide a transparent record of a product's journey from farm to table, ensuring quality and authenticity. Meanwhile, IoT devices like temperature sensors can monitor storage conditions in real-time, alerting managers if temperatures exceed safe levels, preventing food spoilage.

2. Digital Ordering and Payment Systems

The rise of digital ordering and payment systems has significantly changed how customers interact with F&B businesses. These systems streamline the ordering process, improve accuracy, and cater to the growing demand for contactless experiences.

Online and Mobile Ordering:

Many customers prefer ordering food online, whether for delivery or pickup. Mobile apps and online platforms provide customers with an easy way to browse menus, customize orders, and pay in advance. This technology enhances customer convenience and reduces strain on front-line staff, as fewer orders need to be taken in person or over the phone.

Delivery Partnerships: Many F&B businesses partner with third-party delivery apps like Uber Eats, Grubhub, and DoorDash to expand their reach and attract new customers. These platforms make it easy for customers to discover new restaurants, but they also collect valuable customer data that can be used for targeted marketing.

Self-Service Kiosks:

Self-service kiosks, often found in fast-casual and quick-service restaurants, allow customers to place their orders directly on a screen. These kiosks are especially effective in high-traffic areas where they reduce wait times and allow customers to explore menu options at their own pace. Kiosks also enable upselling and cross-selling, as the screen can suggest add-ons based on customer selections.

Contactless Payment Systems:

The COVID-19 pandemic accelerated the adoption of contactless payment options. Today, customers can use mobile wallets, QR codes, or tap-to-pay cards to complete transactions without physically interacting with a payment terminal. This not only improves hygiene but also speeds up the checkout process, enhancing the customer experience.

Table-Top Ordering and Payment Tablets:

In many full-service restaurants, table-top tablets allow customers to place orders, request refills, and pay their bill without needing a server. This technology can streamline service, increase table turnover, and reduce labor costs while providing customers with a sense of control over their dining experience.

3. Use of Data Analytics and AI in F&B

Data analytics and artificial intelligence (AI) have become powerful tools in the F&B industry, providing insights into customer behavior, optimizing inventory, enhancing marketing efforts, and even improving menu planning.

Customer Insights and Personalization:

Data analytics tools allow F&B businesses to gather information on customer preferences, purchase histories, and demographics. By analyzing this data, businesses can personalize their offerings to suit individual preferences. For example, if data shows that a particular customer frequently orders vegan options, targeted marketing can be used to inform them of new vegan items or promotions.

Inventory Optimization:

AI and predictive analytics can be used to forecast demand based on historical sales data, seasonal trends, and even local events. By accurately predicting demand, businesses can adjust inventory levels accordingly, reducing waste and ensuring popular items are always available.

Menu Engineering and Optimization:

Data-driven menu engineering helps F&B establishments optimize their menus for profitability and popularity. By analyzing sales data, managers can identify which items are the most profitable and adjust pricing or remove items that aren't performing well. This approach maximizes profits and aligns menu offerings with customer preferences.

AI in Dynamic Pricing:

Dynamic pricing, commonly used in industries like airlines and hotels, is now gaining traction in F&B. AI algorithms can adjust prices based on demand, time of day, or seasonality. For instance, prices for popular items may increase during peak times or special events, helping businesses maximize revenue.

Enhancing Customer Service with AI Chatbots:

AI-powered chatbots are increasingly used by F&B businesses, particularly for online ordering and customer support. These chatbots can handle customer inquiries, take orders, and even suggest menu items, providing a seamless experience while reducing the workload for staff. Chatbots are available 24/7, which is especially valuable for handling customer questions outside of business hours.

Predictive Maintenance for Kitchen Equipment:

IoT sensors and AI-powered predictive maintenance systems can monitor kitchen equipment and identify potential issues before they cause breakdowns. This helps prevent costly disruptions and extends the lifespan of kitchen assets by ensuring they are maintained proactively.

Supply Chain Transparency and Blockchain:

Blockchain technology provides a decentralized and transparent record of transactions within the supply chain. In the F&B industry, blockchain can help verify the source of ingredients, authenticate organic or fair-trade certifications, and track a product's journey from farm to table. This transparency can build customer trust and add value to brands that prioritize quality and ethical sourcing.

Technology is transforming the food and beverage industry by enhancing efficiency, improving customer experience, and enabling data-driven decision-making. Digital ordering and payment systems cater to the demand for convenience, speed, and hygiene, while data analytics and AI provide powerful insights that allow businesses to personalize offerings, streamline inventory, and optimize pricing. As these technologies continue to evolve, F&B businesses that embrace them will be better positioned to meet customer expectations, improve profitability, and drive sustainable growth. This chapter highlights the importance of staying up-to-date with technological advancements and adopting tools that support operational efficiency, customer satisfaction, and long-term success in a highly competitive industry.

Chapter 15: Sustainability in the Food and Beverage Industry

Sustainability in the food and beverage (F&B) industry has become a crucial focus as businesses aim to address the environmental impact of their operations. This chapter explores sustainable sourcing practices, waste reduction and energy efficiency strategies, and the ethical responsibilities that form the foundation of corporate social responsibility (CSR) in the industry. Understanding these aspects is essential for F&B businesses to reduce their ecological footprint, respond to growing consumer demand for eco-friendly practices, and ensure a sustainable future.

1. Sustainable Sourcing Practices

Sustainable sourcing emphasizes procuring ingredients and materials in a way that minimizes environmental impact and supports ethical practices. This involves focusing on several key principles, including the responsible use of natural resources, fair labor practices, and support for local communities.

Locally Sourced Ingredients:

By sourcing ingredients locally, F&B businesses reduce the carbon footprint associated with transportation. Locally sourced ingredients also support regional farmers and suppliers, contributing to the local economy and encouraging sustainable agricultural practices. Additionally, fresh, local ingredients often have better quality and fewer preservatives, aligning with the trend toward healthier, natural foods.

Ethical and Fair-Trade Products:

Ethical sourcing means considering the working conditions and wages of those involved in the production process. Fair-trade products, like coffee, chocolate, and tea, ensure that farmers receive fair compensation and work under safe conditions. Supporting fair trade helps to combat exploitation, and fair-trade certification provides transparency for consumers who value ethical sourcing.

Environmentally Friendly Packaging:

Packaging is a significant contributor to waste in the F&B industry. Sustainable sourcing includes using environmentally friendly materials, such as recyclable, biodegradable, or compostable packaging. Reducing single-use plastics, opting for reusable containers, and sourcing materials with a lower environmental impact are essential for businesses aiming to achieve sustainability.

Supporting Biodiversity and Conservation:

Sustainable sourcing practices should avoid overharvesting and prioritize preserving biodiversity. F&B businesses can partner with suppliers who practice sustainable farming and fishing, ensuring that natural ecosystems are protected and that endangered species are not negatively affected by sourcing practices.

2. Waste Reduction and Energy Efficiency

Minimizing waste and improving energy efficiency are essential components of sustainable operations. From managing food waste to investing in energy-efficient equipment, F&B businesses can adopt a variety of practices to reduce their environmental impact.

Food Waste Management:

Food waste is a significant issue within the F&B industry. Many businesses are now adopting waste reduction strategies, such as donating excess food, composting, and repurposing ingredients.

Reducing food waste not only conserves resources but also aligns with consumer expectations, as many customers are increasingly aware of the environmental impacts of waste. Technology, like inventory tracking systems and AI-driven demand forecasting, can also help F&B businesses accurately manage stock levels, reducing spoilage.

Energy-Efficient Equipment:

Energy-efficient appliances and equipment, such as LED lighting, high-efficiency ovens, and refrigeration units, can reduce energy consumption. Energy-efficient equipment often has a higher initial cost but leads to long-term savings on utility bills and a reduction in greenhouse gas emissions. Businesses can also consider retrofitting existing facilities to reduce their energy use, such as improving insulation or installing programmable thermostats.

Water Conservation:

The F&B industry is a significant consumer of water, especially in food preparation and cleaning processes. Businesses can adopt water-saving practices, such as using low-flow faucets, recycling greywater for non-potable uses, and training staff on water conservation techniques. Monitoring and optimizing water use not only helps to lower utility costs but also supports environmental conservation.

Recycling and Composting Programs:

Recycling and composting programs help F&B businesses minimize the waste that ends up in landfills. Recycling materials such as glass, paper, and plastic, and composting organic waste, can significantly reduce the environmental impact of daily operations. Some businesses go a step further by reusing food waste to create new products, such as turning food scraps into broths, sauces, or even animal feed.

3. Ethical Considerations and Corporate Social Responsibility (CSR)

Corporate social responsibility (CSR) in the F&B industry extends beyond environmental impact to encompass fair labor practices, community engagement, and ethical business practices. A strong CSR framework is essential for businesses aiming to build trust, maintain a positive public image, and respond to consumer expectations for ethical behavior.

Employee Welfare and Fair Labor Practices:

Ethical considerations in CSR start with fair treatment of employees. This includes offering fair wages, ensuring safe working conditions, and providing opportunities for training and advancement. Labor practices should extend to the broader supply chain, ensuring that suppliers also adhere to ethical standards regarding worker rights, fair pay, and health and safety.

Transparency and Accountability:

Transparency about sourcing, production practices, and sustainability efforts helps F&B businesses build trust with consumers. Many businesses are opting to share information about where ingredients come from, how they are processed, and what measures are taken to ensure sustainability. Additionally, third-party certifications and environmental reports enhance accountability, as they provide an unbiased assessment of a business's practices.

Community Involvement and Support:

Many F&B businesses are adopting CSR initiatives that support their local communities, such as sourcing locally, engaging in charitable donations, and sponsoring community events. Some companies also support food banks or offer educational programs on nutrition and sustainable food practices. By fostering positive community relationships, businesses strengthen their brand reputation and align themselves with social responsibility.

Adopting Ethical Animal Welfare Standards:

For F&B businesses involved with animal-based products, adhering to high animal welfare standards is essential for CSR. Ethical treatment of animals, such as ensuring humane farming practices and avoiding confinement, resonates with consumers who are increasingly concerned about animal welfare. Many consumers are willing to pay more for products labeled as free-range, organic, or cruelty-free, which also enhances brand image.

Implementing Green Initiatives:

Adopting green practices, such as reducing energy consumption, eliminating single-use plastics, and minimizing food waste, helps to protect the environment and support sustainability goals. Many businesses are moving towards carbon neutrality, a commitment to offsetting or reducing their carbon emissions, which appeals to environmentally conscious consumers.

Sustainability in the food and beverage industry requires a comprehensive approach that incorporates sustainable sourcing, waste reduction, energy efficiency, and ethical responsibility. As consumers increasingly prioritize environmental and social responsibility, F&B businesses that adopt sustainable practices are better positioned for long-term success. By incorporating sustainable sourcing practices, reducing waste, enhancing energy efficiency, and fostering ethical standards, businesses not only contribute to environmental protection but also build trust and loyalty among customers. The role of sustainability in F&B is crucial for future growth, customer satisfaction, and global environmental stewardship.

Chapter 16: Franchising and Expansion in Food and Beverage

Franchising and expansion have become popular strategies for food and beverage (F&B) businesses aiming to scale their brand and increase market reach. This chapter explores the advantages and disadvantages of franchising, the essential steps for establishing a franchise, and effective international expansion strategies. By understanding these aspects, F&B businesses can make informed decisions on how best to grow their operations locally and globally.

1. Pros and Cons of Franchising

Franchising offers a structured model for expansion, allowing F&B businesses to grow rapidly by partnering with franchisees. However, franchising also comes with certain challenges that businesses must consider.

Pros of Franchising:

Scalability and Rapid Growth: Franchising allows a brand to expand quickly without incurring the full cost of opening new locations. Franchisees invest their capital, enabling faster expansion into new regions.

Brand Awareness and Market Penetration: A well-implemented franchise model can enhance brand recognition, especially in new areas. The more locations a brand has, the more visible it becomes, helping it attract a wider customer base.

Lower Financial Risk: Franchising reduces financial risk for the franchisor, as franchisees bear the primary responsibility for the capital investment and day-to-day operations of each location.

Local Expertise: Franchisees bring local market knowledge, allowing the brand to navigate regional customer preferences, regulatory requirements, and competitive dynamics more effectively.

Cons of Franchising:

Loss of Control: Franchisors may lose some control over day-to-day operations, making it challenging to ensure consistent service quality across all franchise locations.

Dependency on Franchisee Performance: The success of a franchise heavily depends on the commitment and capabilities of the franchisees. Poor management by a franchisee can harm the brand's reputation and customer experience.

Legal and Regulatory Complexities: Franchise agreements involve complex legal and regulatory requirements, which vary across regions and countries. Complying with these regulations requires substantial effort and resources.

Shared Profits: While franchising allows for expansion with lower initial capital, it also means sharing profits with franchisees. The franchisor typically receives royalties, which may be lower than potential profits from a company-owned location.

2. Steps to Establish a Franchise

Establishing a successful franchise requires a structured approach to ensure brand consistency, franchisee support, and operational efficiency. Here are the key steps for establishing an F&B franchise:

Step 1: Develop a Franchise Business Model:

Before franchising, the business should develop a replicable and scalable model. This includes creating a comprehensive operations manual that outlines every aspect of the business—from customer service to inventory management. The business model should also detail revenue-sharing structures, franchise fees, royalties, and expected profit margins.

Step 2: Protect Intellectual Property:

Branding, recipes, and operational processes are critical assets for an F&B business. Protecting these elements through trademarks, patents (if applicable), and copyrights is essential to prevent unauthorized use by franchisees or competitors.

Step 3: Establish Franchise Agreements:

The franchise agreement is a legally binding document that outlines the roles, responsibilities, and expectations of both the franchisor and franchisee. It should cover terms such as franchise duration, renewal options, training requirements, branding guidelines, and conditions for terminating the franchise.

Step 4: Provide Comprehensive Training and Support:

Training programs help franchisees understand brand standards, customer service protocols, and daily operational processes. Ongoing support, including marketing, supplier relationships, and business analytics, is essential to help franchisees succeed.

Step 5: Develop Marketing and Brand Guidelines:

Consistent branding is crucial for building customer trust. Franchisors should establish guidelines on marketing, social media, store layout, signage, and employee uniforms to maintain brand consistency across all locations.

Step 6: Select Franchisees Carefully:

The selection process should evaluate potential franchisees' financial resources, industry experience, and commitment to brand values. Choosing the right franchisees minimizes risks and enhances the likelihood of successful partnerships.

Step 7: Monitor and Evaluate Franchise Performance:

Regular monitoring helps ensure that franchisees adhere to brand standards and performance expectations. Franchisors should develop performance metrics and conduct regular audits to address issues promptly and provide constructive feedback.

3. International Expansion Strategies

Expanding internationally opens up new revenue streams and growth opportunities but requires careful planning and adaptation. Here are some strategies for F&B businesses looking to expand globally:

Market Research and Localization:

Before entering a new market, it's essential to conduct thorough research to understand local consumer preferences, dietary habits, and cultural nuances. Localization—such as adapting the menu or adjusting marketing messages—helps businesses cater to regional tastes and preferences, making the brand more appealing to local consumers.

Selecting the Right Entry Mode:

F&B businesses can enter international markets through various methods, such as joint ventures, partnerships, wholly-owned subsidiaries, or master franchise agreements. Each mode has different levels of control, investment requirements, and risk. For instance, a joint venture with a local partner can help navigate complex regulatory environments and leverage local market knowledge.

Adapting to Regulatory Requirements:

Different countries have unique regulations regarding food safety, labeling, labor laws, and environmental standards. Compliance with these regulations is crucial to avoid legal issues. Working with local legal experts can help businesses navigate regulatory complexities and ensure that their operations are compliant.

Building a Robust Supply Chain:

An effective supply chain is essential for maintaining product quality and consistency across locations. Businesses should evaluate potential suppliers, distribution channels, and logistics providers to ensure timely and cost-effective delivery of ingredients and other materials. Partnering with local suppliers can also enhance supply chain efficiency and sustainability.

Brand Consistency and Quality Control:

Maintaining brand consistency across international locations is critical to preserving the brand's reputation. Implementing strict quality control measures, such as regular audits and mystery shopper programs, helps ensure that international franchisees adhere to brand standards.

Leveraging Digital Marketing for Global Reach:

Digital marketing allows brands to build awareness before entering a new market. Social media platforms, influencer partnerships, and online advertising can generate buzz and attract a loyal customer base. Additionally, online ordering and delivery options allow customers to access products even before physical locations are established.

Franchising and international expansion offer significant growth opportunities for F&B businesses, enabling them to reach new markets and increase profitability. However, both approaches require careful planning and a strong commitment to maintaining brand consistency, quality standards, and compliance with local regulations. By understanding the pros and cons of franchising, following a structured approach to franchise development, and employing effective international expansion strategies, F&B businesses can successfully navigate the complexities of growth and scale their brand on a global level.

Chapter 17: Legal and Regulatory Compliance

Legal and regulatory compliance is a cornerstone of the food and beverage (F&B) industry, impacting everything from product labeling to employee rights. This chapter explores the critical areas of compliance, including food labeling and packaging laws, alcohol licensing and regulations, and employment and labor laws. Adhering to these requirements is essential for avoiding penalties, maintaining brand integrity, and fostering a safe and fair workplace.

1. Food Labeling and Packaging Laws

Food labeling and packaging laws protect consumers by ensuring they have accurate information about what they are purchasing and consuming. These laws differ by country but often cover common elements such as ingredients, allergens, nutritional information, and expiration dates.

Ingredient and Allergen Disclosure: Most countries require that all ingredients in a food product be clearly listed on the packaging, with specific emphasis on potential allergens (e.g., nuts, dairy, gluten). In the United States, the Food Allergen Labeling and Consumer Protection Act mandates that allergens be highlighted in bold or listed in a separate section to prevent allergic reactions and protect consumer health.

Nutritional Information: Many regions require nutritional facts on food packaging, including calories, fats, carbohydrates, sugars, and protein content. This information helps consumers make informed dietary choices and aligns with health initiatives that encourage reduced sugar and fat consumption.

Country of Origin Labeling: Some countries mandate that food labels include the origin of the product or its primary ingredients. This information is particularly important for consumers seeking locally sourced products or those with specific ethical preferences, such as fair-trade or sustainably sourced goods.

Expiration and 'Best Before' Dates: Ensuring product safety also involves displaying clear expiration and "best before" dates, as these indicators inform consumers when a product is no longer safe or of optimal quality. Compliance with these labeling requirements minimizes the risk of consumers inadvertently consuming spoiled or unsafe food.

2. Alcohol Licensing and Regulations

The sale and distribution of alcoholic beverages in the F&B industry are tightly regulated due to the associated social, health, and safety concerns. Licensing laws and regulations vary widely, and non-compliance can result in severe penalties, including fines, license revocation, or business closure.

Obtaining a License: To legally sell alcohol, F&B establishments must obtain an alcohol license, which can vary depending on the type of establishment, hours of operation, and type of alcohol served (e.g., beer, wine, spirits). In some countries, obtaining an alcohol license requires background checks and compliance with local zoning laws.

Compliance with Age Restrictions: Age verification is a core component of alcohol licensing regulations. Most countries have a legal drinking age, often between 18 and 21 years, and businesses must verify the age of customers purchasing or consuming alcohol on their premises. Failure to comply with these age restrictions can lead to fines, license suspension, or loss of operating rights.

Limits on Hours of Sale: In some jurisdictions, regulations limit the hours when alcohol can be sold or served, such as prohibiting sales after midnight. These restrictions are intended to reduce alcohol-related incidents and maintain public safety.

Staff Training and Certification: Many countries require staff handling alcohol to undergo specific training programs, such as the Responsible Beverage Service (RBS) certification in the United States. These programs teach employees how to prevent over-serving, manage intoxicated patrons, and understand the legal implications of serving alcohol.

3. Employment and Labor Laws in Food and Beverage

Employment and labor laws are designed to protect the rights and welfare of workers, and they cover critical areas such as minimum wage, working hours, workplace safety, and employee benefits. Compliance with these laws not only ensures a fair working environment but also fosters employee satisfaction and reduces turnover.

Minimum Wage and Compensation: Minimum wage laws mandate a baseline pay for employees, which can vary by country, state, or even city. In many cases, the F&B industry also includes tipped employees, whose base wage may be lower, with the expectation that tips will supplement their income. Employers must ensure that employees earn at least the minimum wage, even if their tips fall short.

Working Hours and Overtime Pay: Labor laws often regulate working hours, including daily and weekly maximums, as well as mandatory breaks. In many countries, employees are entitled to overtime pay for hours worked beyond a standard threshold, often at a rate of 1.5 times their regular pay. Compliance with these rules is crucial to avoid costly fines and ensure employee well-being.

Health and Safety Regulations: Health and safety laws require that workplaces, including kitchens and food preparation areas, be safe for employees. Compliance involves maintaining sanitary conditions, providing safety training, and ensuring that employees have access to proper protective equipment. For example, in the United States, the Occupational Safety and Health Administration (OSHA) sets safety standards that all F&B businesses must follow.

Anti-Discrimination and Equal Opportunity: Labor laws prohibit discrimination based on race, gender, religion, age, disability, and other factors. F&B businesses must provide equal opportunities to all employees and applicants and prevent workplace harassment. Violating anti-discrimination laws can lead to lawsuits and damage the business's reputation.

Employee Benefits and Rights: Many regions mandate specific employee benefits, such as paid sick leave, family leave, and health insurance. In addition to meeting legal requirements, offering competitive benefits can enhance employee retention and attract top talent. Compliance with benefits laws also demonstrates a business's commitment to supporting its employees.

Legal and regulatory compliance in the F&B industry is multifaceted, encompassing food labeling, alcohol licensing, and labor laws. By adhering to these regulations, businesses protect their customers, employees, and brand reputation. Compliance also fosters trust with consumers, who rely on transparent information, ethical sourcing, and safe practices. As laws evolve, F&B businesses must stay informed and adapt to remain compliant in a highly regulated industry.

Chapter 18: Trends in the Food and Beverage Industry

The food and beverage industry is constantly evolving, driven by changing consumer preferences, advances in technology, and a growing awareness of health, sustainability, and ethics. In this chapter, we will explore some of the key trends that are shaping the industry today, including plant-based and alternative proteins, organic and locally sourced ingredients, and innovations in food packaging and delivery. Each of these trends is influencing how food is produced, marketed, and consumed, and businesses in the F&B industry must adapt to remain competitive and meet the demands of modern consumers.

1. Plant-Based and Alternative Proteins

One of the most significant trends in the food and beverage industry in recent years is the rise of plant-based and alternative proteins. As consumers become more health-conscious, environmentally aware, and ethically motivated, the demand for plant-based foods and meat alternatives has surged. This trend reflects a broader shift towards plant-based diets and the desire to reduce animal product consumption.

Health and Wellness Motivation: Many consumers are adopting plant-based diets for health reasons. Plant-based foods tend to be lower in saturated fats and cholesterol, and they provide higher amounts of fiber and certain vitamins. This shift toward plant-based eating is supported by research indicating that plant-based diets can reduce the risk of chronic diseases such as heart disease, diabetes, and certain cancers.

Environmental Impact: The environmental benefits of plant-based diets are also a major driver of this trend. The production of plant-based foods generally has a lower environmental impact than animal agriculture. Livestock farming is a significant contributor to greenhouse gas emissions, deforestation, and water usage. By switching to plant-based proteins, consumers can reduce their carbon footprint and help mitigate climate change.

Innovation in Plant-Based Products: The market for plant-based proteins has expanded beyond just vegetarians and vegans. Companies like Impossible Foods and Beyond Meat have revolutionized the plant-based protein market by creating alternatives that closely mimic the taste, texture, and appearance of animal-based meat. These innovations have made plant-based proteins more accessible to a mainstream audience. Plant-based burgers, sausages, and chicken substitutes are now common on restaurant menus and in grocery stores, catering to both plant-based eaters and flexitarians—those who reduce their meat consumption without eliminating it entirely.

Alternative Protein Sources: In addition to soy, peas, and other traditional plant-based proteins, there is growing interest in novel alternative proteins such as insect protein, lab-grown meat, and algae-based proteins. These alternative sources offer high-quality protein with lower environmental impact and may play an important role in feeding a growing global population.

Insect Protein: Insects are a highly efficient protein source with a minimal environmental footprint. Companies are developing insect-based protein powders and snacks to offer a sustainable alternative to traditional meat. Crickets, mealworms, and grasshoppers are some of the most commonly used insects in food production.

Lab-Grown Meat: Lab-grown or cultured meat is produced by cultivating animal cells in a lab rather than raising and slaughtering animals. Although still in the early stages of development, lab-grown meat holds promise for addressing ethical concerns surrounding animal cruelty and the environmental impact of traditional meat production. Companies like Eat Just and Memphis Meats are at the forefront of this innovation.

Algae-Based Proteins: Algae is another alternative protein source that is gaining attention. Algae-based protein products, such as spirulina and chlorella, are packed with essential amino acids, making them a valuable addition to plant-based diets. These proteins can be used in smoothies, protein bars, and supplements, offering a sustainable, nutrient-dense alternative to animal proteins.

2. Organic and Locally Sourced Ingredients

Consumers are increasingly interested in knowing where their food comes from, how it is grown, and the impact of its production on the environment. As a result, there has been a significant rise in demand for organic and locally sourced ingredients in food and beverage production. This trend reflects a growing desire for transparency, sustainability, and health-conscious choices.

Organic Foods: Organic food production avoids the use of synthetic pesticides, fertilizers, and genetically modified organisms (GMOs). Organic farming practices are designed to promote biodiversity, soil health, and sustainable land use. For many consumers, organic products are seen as a healthier and more environmentally friendly option compared to conventionally grown foods.

The organic food market has grown significantly in recent years, with more consumers willing to pay a premium for products that are certified organic. This includes organic fruits and vegetables, dairy products, grains, and meat. Retailers are also expanding their organic offerings to meet consumer demand, with organic sections becoming commonplace in supermarkets.

Health Benefits: Organic foods are often perceived as healthier because they are free from synthetic chemicals and pesticides. Some studies suggest that organic foods may contain higher levels of certain nutrients, such as antioxidants, compared to conventionally grown counterparts. This perception is fueling the demand for organic products among health-conscious consumers.

Environmental Impact: Organic farming methods are considered more environmentally sustainable because they rely on crop rotation, composting, and other natural practices to improve soil health and reduce the need for chemical inputs. Organic farming also tends to use fewer resources like water and energy, making it a more eco-friendly choice.

Locally Sourced Ingredients: In addition to organic products, consumers are increasingly seeking locally sourced ingredients. Local sourcing refers to foods that are grown or produced within a specific region, typically within a 100-mile radius of the point of sale or consumption. The demand for local ingredients is driven by several factors:

Support for Local Economies: By purchasing locally sourced products, consumers are helping to support local farmers, artisans, and food producers. This trend promotes community-based economies and strengthens the local food system.

Freshness and Quality: Locally sourced ingredients are often fresher and more flavorful than those that are transported long distances.

When produce is grown closer to home, it can be harvested at the peak of ripeness and delivered to market quickly, ensuring better taste and nutritional value.

Sustainability: Local sourcing reduces the carbon footprint associated with long-distance food transportation, leading to lower greenhouse gas emissions. This is particularly important as consumers become more concerned with the environmental impact of their food choices.

Farm-to-Table and Sustainable Agriculture: The farm-to-table movement, which emphasizes using fresh, locally sourced ingredients in restaurant menus, has gained popularity in recent years. Many chefs and restaurateurs are sourcing directly from local farms to ensure that their dishes feature the highest-quality, seasonal ingredients. This approach not only supports sustainable agriculture but also promotes transparency and traceability in the food supply chain.

3. Innovations in Food Packaging and Delivery

As the demand for convenience and sustainability continues to grow, innovations in food packaging and delivery are becoming increasingly important. Packaging and delivery methods have a significant impact on the environmental footprint of food products, and businesses are looking for ways to reduce waste, improve functionality, and enhance customer experience.

Sustainable Packaging: Traditional food packaging, such as plastic containers, bottles, and wrappers, has been a major contributor to global plastic pollution. In response, many food and beverage companies are exploring alternative packaging solutions that are more sustainable and environmentally friendly.

Biodegradable and Compostable Packaging: Materials such as plant-based plastics, biodegradable films, and paper packaging are gaining popularity as alternatives to conventional plastic. These materials are designed to break down more quickly in landfills, reducing their impact on the environment.

Edible Packaging: Some companies are experimenting with edible packaging made from materials like seaweed, rice, and other plant-based ingredients. These packaging materials can be consumed along with the product, eliminating the need for disposal altogether.

Glass and Aluminum: Reusable glass and aluminum containers are being used more frequently in the food and beverage industry. These materials are easier to recycle and have a lower environmental impact compared to single-use plastic.

Smart Packaging: Advances in technology are also leading to innovations in smart packaging. Smart packaging includes features such as QR codes, temperature sensors, and RFID (radio frequency identification) tags that provide consumers with real-time information about the freshness, storage conditions, and origin of their food. This kind of packaging can enhance customer trust and improve the overall food safety and supply chain transparency.

Food Delivery and E-Commerce: The rise of food delivery services has been one of the defining trends in recent years, particularly with the growth of platforms like Uber Eats, DoorDash, and Grubhub. These platforms allow consumers to order food from their favorite restaurants and have it delivered directly to their doorsteps. In response, restaurants and food businesses have had to adapt their operations to accommodate delivery orders.

Ghost Kitchens: Ghost kitchens are commercial kitchen spaces used exclusively for food delivery. These kitchens allow businesses to optimize their operations by focusing on delivery without the need for a physical storefront. The ghost kitchen model has become increasingly popular as food delivery demand continues to grow.

Contactless Delivery: The COVID-19 pandemic accelerated the demand for contactless delivery options, and this trend is likely to continue. Contactless delivery options, such as curbside pickup and delivery via autonomous vehicles, are becoming more common as consumers seek safer, more efficient ways to receive their food orders.

Subscription Meal Services: Meal kit services like Blue Apron, HelloFresh, and others have gained popularity as consumers seek convenient, pre-portioned meals delivered to their homes. These services provide the ingredients and recipes needed to prepare meals at home, catering to a variety of dietary preferences and lifestyles.

The food and beverage industry is evolving rapidly, shaped by trends that emphasize health, sustainability, and innovation. Plant-based and alternative proteins are driving changes in consumer diets, while organic and locally sourced ingredients offer a more

Chapter 19: Event Catering and Special Services

Event catering and special services are a vital segment of the food and beverage industry, encompassing everything from intimate gatherings to large-scale events like weddings, corporate functions, and festivals. Successful event catering requires meticulous planning, a deep understanding of customer needs, and a streamlined approach to logistics and service. This chapter will explore the basics of catering operations, strategies for handling large events and creating customized menus, and the critical role of logistics and planning for special occasions.

1. Basics of Catering Operations

Catering involves the preparation, presentation, and service of food and beverages for clients and their guests at a particular venue or event. Unlike restaurant dining, which has a controlled environment, catering often requires transporting food to off-site locations and working in diverse settings with different logistics and requirements.

Types of Catering: Catering services can vary widely, including options such as:

On-Premise Catering: Where food is prepared and served at a venue, such as a banquet hall or hotel, with access to a fully equipped kitchen.

Off-Premise Catering: Food is prepared at the catering company's kitchen and transported to the event location, which may not have a full kitchen.

Corporate Catering: Tailored for business events such as conferences, product launches, and meetings. The focus is often on convenience, efficiency, and professional presentation.

Social Event Catering: For occasions like weddings, birthdays, anniversaries, and holiday parties, where menus and service style are often customized to meet the needs of the client.

Menu Planning: Menu planning is fundamental in catering, balancing variety, seasonality, dietary restrictions, and the specific theme or style of the event. The menu should appeal to a broad range of tastes and dietary needs while ensuring that dishes can be produced and served efficiently at scale.

Food Preparation and Safety: Caterers must adhere to stringent food safety standards, as off-premise catering presents unique challenges in maintaining the right temperatures and handling food safely during transport. This includes using specialized equipment such as insulated containers, chafing dishes, and portable refrigeration units to prevent contamination.

Staffing and Training: Catering teams typically include chefs, servers, bartenders, event coordinators, and support staff. All staff members need to be trained in food handling, customer service, and time management, as catering events often involve high-pressure situations requiring a coordinated team effort.

2. Handling Large Events and Customized Menus

Large events, such as corporate galas, charity fundraisers, and weddings, present unique challenges for catering companies. These events demand customized menus, efficient service, and coordination with other event professionals to ensure a seamless experience.

Customized Menu Development: Many clients seek personalized menu options to make their event memorable and reflect their unique tastes and values. Catering companies work closely with clients to design customized menus that may include specific cultural dishes, themed options, or dietary accommodations.

Specialty and Themed Menus: For themed events, such as a tropical wedding or a formal business banquet, the menu often reflects the theme. This could include regional cuisines, unique presentation styles, or matching cocktails.

Dietary Considerations: With increasing awareness of dietary needs, caterers must be prepared to offer options for guests with allergies or preferences, such as gluten-free, vegan, or low-carb dishes.

Service Styles: Different events require different service styles, and choosing the right one is essential to meet the client's needs and the event's tone.

Plated Service: Guests are served individual plates by staff. This style is ideal for formal events and provides greater portion control.

Buffet Service: Guests serve themselves from a central buffet. This style is common for larger, more casual events, allowing for a wider variety of food.

Family Style: Dishes are served in large portions at each table, and guests help themselves. This style creates a communal, shared dining experience.

Stations: Food stations or live cooking stations offer diverse options where guests can choose customized dishes, such as pasta bars, carving stations, or sushi stations.

Managing Large Guest Counts: Large events require efficient planning to manage high guest volumes. This involves:

Accurate Headcount and Inventory Control: Working closely with the event organizer to obtain an accurate headcount and ensuring sufficient ingredients, dishes, and cutlery are on hand.

Scalable Food Production: Preparing dishes that can be cooked in bulk and still maintain quality. Some items may be pre-cooked and finished on-site to optimize workflow.

Timing and Flow: Timing is critical in large events. Caterers must have detailed schedules for meal preparation, serving times, and clean-up to avoid delays or bottlenecks.

3. Logistics and Planning for Special Occasions

Logistics and planning are crucial in catering, especially for special occasions where the stakes are high. Clients expect flawless service, which demands efficient coordination across all aspects of the catering operation.

Event Site Assessment: Caterers often conduct site visits before the event to assess the layout, available facilities, and any restrictions. They evaluate:

Kitchen Space: Checking if the site has kitchen facilities, power outlets, and space for food prep and storage.

Access and Setup Areas: Identifying areas where catering trucks can unload, and where to set up food stations, bars, and dining areas.

Power and Utilities: Ensuring there are adequate power sources for cooking equipment and lighting, especially in outdoor venues.

Scheduling and Coordination: Timing and coordination with other event professionals—such as florists, decorators, and audio-visual teams—are essential for seamless execution. A detailed timeline should include:

Setup Time: Arriving early to set up kitchens, tables, and equipment.

Food Preparation and Plating: Preparing food based on the planned serving times, ensuring dishes are fresh and ready on schedule.

Service Coordination: Aligning with the event's program, such as speeches or ceremonies, to serve food at appropriate intervals.

Cleanup and Breakdown: Post-event cleanup, including removing trash, packing up equipment, and restoring the venue to its original state.

Transportation and Equipment: Logistics also involve transporting food, equipment, and staff to the event location. For off-premise catering, specialized equipment like insulated containers, portable burners, and refrigeration units is often necessary to keep food at the right temperature during transit. The use of trucks, vans, or even mobile kitchens may be required for large events or remote locations.

Contingency Planning: Catering for special occasions means preparing for unexpected issues, such as weather changes, power outages, or ingredient shortages. Contingency plans might include backup equipment, alternative dishes, and rain covers for outdoor events.

4. Trends in Event Catering and Special Services

The catering industry has seen several innovations and trends that enhance the guest experience and cater to evolving customer preferences.

Eco-Friendly and Sustainable Catering: Many clients are now seeking sustainable options in catering. This includes using organic, locally sourced ingredients, minimizing waste, and opting for reusable or compostable serving ware. Some caterers even offer zero-waste event options, where all materials are recyclable or compostable.

Interactive and DIY Stations: Interactive food stations, such as build-your-own tacos, sushi rolling stations, or custom dessert bars, provide an engaging experience for guests. DIY stations encourage interaction, allowing guests to personalize their dishes.

Technology in Catering: Technology plays an increasing role in streamlining catering operations. Mobile ordering apps, digital inventory systems, and real-time communication tools improve coordination, reduce errors, and enhance the customer experience.

Global and Fusion Cuisines: With globalization, there is a rising demand for diverse and fusion cuisines in catering. Clients may request a blend of different cuisines or authentic dishes from specific cultures, giving guests a unique culinary experience.

Health-Conscious Catering Options: More clients are interested in catering options that include healthy, low-calorie, or superfood-rich meals. Caterers offer options like smoothie bars, plant-based menus, and low-sugar desserts to accommodate health-conscious guests.

Event catering and special services require a unique blend of culinary skills, operational efficiency, and customer service. From managing large-scale events to offering customized menus and handling logistics, catering businesses must ensure that every aspect is planned and executed to perfection. By understanding client needs, incorporating industry trends, and focusing on quality and service, catering companies can create memorable experiences for their clients and set themselves apart in a competitive industry.

Chapter 20: Customer Experience in Food and Beverage

The customer experience (CX) in the food and beverage industry extends beyond the quality of food and service. It encompasses every interaction a customer has with a business, from the moment they learn about it to the time they leave the establishment. Successful food and beverage businesses prioritize a memorable and positive experience by understanding the customer journey, enhancing ambiance and decor, and actively gathering and using customer feedback.

1. Understanding the Customer Journey and Touchpoints

The customer journey in food and beverage involves every step a customer takes, starting with their discovery of a business and ending with their post-visit interactions. Recognizing each touchpoint and tailoring it to enhance the experience can significantly impact customer satisfaction and loyalty.

Awareness and Discovery: The journey typically begins when potential customers become aware of the establishment. This may happen through marketing, word-of-mouth, or online reviews. First impressions are essential, so maintaining a strong online presence and reputation is critical.

Social Media and Online Reviews: Today's customers often search online before visiting a restaurant or bar. Platforms like Instagram, Google, Yelp, and TripAdvisor are powerful tools for attracting new customers. Positive reviews and appealing photos of the ambiance and dishes play a big role in shaping perceptions.

Website and Menu Accessibility: Many customers check websites for menus, hours of operation, or reservations. Ensuring a mobile-friendly, easy-to-navigate website with up-to-date information helps customers in their decision-making process.

Arrival and First Impressions: The experience as customers enter the establishment is crucial. Greeting them warmly, providing clear signage, and having clean, organized spaces can make customers feel welcome and comfortable.

Valet and Parking: For larger or urban locations, providing easy access to parking or valet services can be a deciding factor for customers.

Host Interaction: The greeting from a host or receptionist is an important touchpoint. A friendly and efficient greeting, especially when the establishment is busy, leaves a positive first impression.

Dining Experience: The heart of the customer journey is the dining experience itself, including interactions with staff, the quality of food and beverages, and the overall ambiance. The server's knowledge of the menu, ability to make recommendations, and attentiveness are central to customer satisfaction.

Order and Wait Time: Efficient ordering systems and reasonable wait times contribute to a positive dining experience. Communicating accurately about wait times or order delays can help manage expectations.

Customer Comfort and Personalization: Making customers feel at ease is key. Remembering their preferences, offering dietary modifications, or accommodating special occasions like birthdays and anniversaries create a personal touch that customers appreciate.

Post-Dining Interaction: The customer journey does not end once the meal is over. The way the establishment handles the bill, customer departures, and follow-up interactions plays an important role in shaping the entire experience.

Bill Settlement and Gratitude: Offering a smooth and pleasant bill settlement process, and thanking customers genuinely, leaves a lasting positive impression. If they have signed up for a loyalty program, ensure they receive points or benefits for their visit.

Follow-up Engagement: Encouraging customers to leave feedback, join mailing lists, or follow the establishment on social media extends the relationship. Loyalty programs and occasional follow-up offers encourage repeat visits.

2. Enhancing Ambiance and Decor

Ambiance is a defining element in food and beverage establishments. The decor, lighting, layout, music, and even scent contribute to the overall atmosphere, creating a space where customers feel comfortable and engaged. An inviting ambiance can make dining experiences more memorable and influence customers to return.

Setting the Theme and Style: A clear and cohesive theme can make the atmosphere more memorable and reflective of the brand's identity. Whether it's a rustic Italian restaurant, a sleek modern cocktail bar, or a cozy café, creating an aesthetic that matches the brand image is key.

Decor and Interior Design: Wall decor, furniture, table settings, and decorative elements should harmonize with the theme. High-end establishments may invest in bespoke decor or commissioned artwork, while casual settings might focus on comfort and familiarity.

Lighting: Lighting affects the mood considerably. Dim, warm lighting is often used in fine dining and bars to create an intimate atmosphere, while brighter, natural light can suit casual or family-oriented venues. Adjustable lighting can help adapt to different times of day or specific events.

Seating Arrangements and Layout: The arrangement of tables, seating, and walking space affects the flow of the environment and customers' comfort. Different seating arrangements can cater to various types of groups, such as large family gatherings, couples on dates, or solo diners.

Accessibility and Space Utilization: The layout should provide enough space for comfortable movement without overcrowding. Accessibility for all patrons, including those with disabilities, is also essential.

Private and Communal Spaces: Offering diverse seating options—such as private booths, communal tables, or outdoor seating—gives customers the choice to select the setting that suits their occasion best.

Music and Acoustics: Background music enhances the dining experience, with different genres and volumes used to create specific moods. Fine dining establishments may favor low, classical music, while upbeat, contemporary tracks may suit a bustling café.

Noise Control: Proper acoustic design helps manage noise levels, which is essential for customer comfort. Acoustic panels, carpeting, or cushioned chairs can help absorb sound in busy establishments, preventing loud echoes or clamor.

Scent and Cleanliness: Scent is an often-overlooked aspect of ambiance. The aroma of freshly brewed coffee in a café, or the scent of herbs and spices in a restaurant, can enhance the dining experience. Cleanliness is also crucial for both ambiance and health safety, from tables and floors to restrooms and food preparation areas.

3. Gathering and Using Customer Feedback

Customer feedback is invaluable for understanding how to improve the overall experience, recognizing what customers appreciate, and identifying areas that need attention. Proactively gathering feedback and using it to make improvements demonstrates a commitment to customer satisfaction.

Methods of Collecting Feedback: There are several ways to gather customer opinions, each with its own strengths. Offering multiple feedback channels encourages diverse customers to share their views.

Surveys and Comment Cards: Providing short surveys or comment cards at the end of a meal gives customers a quick way to share their thoughts. Digital surveys, sent via email or accessed through a QR code, allow customers to respond at their convenience.

Online Reviews and Social Media: Encouraging customers to leave reviews on platforms like Google, Yelp, or social media helps the business gain exposure and receive feedback. Monitoring these channels allows businesses to respond to reviews and address both praise and complaints.

Loyalty Programs and Apps: Loyalty programs often incorporate feedback systems, where customers can rate their experience directly in the app or through email prompts after their visit.

Analyzing Feedback for Insights: Feedback can reveal trends, preferences, and recurring issues. Using data analytics, businesses can track metrics like customer satisfaction scores, identify popular menu items, or pinpoint service issues that need addressing.

Categorizing Feedback: Sorting feedback by themes, such as service quality, food taste, ambiance, or price, helps prioritize areas that require improvement.

Identifying Trends and Patterns: Recurrent feedback about particular aspects—like portion sizes, wait times, or menu preferences—can indicate where adjustments are needed.

Implementing Changes Based on Feedback: Taking actionable steps based on customer feedback not only improves the business but also shows customers that their opinions matter. Establishments can adjust menu items, update decor, or retrain staff to address specific concerns or suggestions.

Training and Staff Development: Negative feedback about service often points to training gaps. Additional training on customer service etiquette or improving communication skills can enhance service quality.

Menu and Ambiance Adjustments: Feedback related to food preferences or ambiance can lead to practical changes, like introducing new dishes, redesigning the space, or adjusting lighting and music.

Following Up with Customers: Showing appreciation to customers who provide feedback reinforces the relationship and encourages repeat visits. Thanking them with personalized emails, discount codes, or loyalty points helps build loyalty and demonstrates responsiveness.

Customer experience in the food and beverage industry is multi-faceted, encompassing the entire journey a customer takes, from initial discovery to post-visit follow-ups. By understanding and enhancing each touchpoint, creating an inviting ambiance, and valuing customer feedback, businesses can foster a loyal customer base and stand out in a competitive market. The ability to continuously improve and adapt to customer needs is central to thriving in today's dynamic food and beverage landscape.

Chapter 21: Crisis Management in Food and Beverage

In the food and beverage industry, crisis management is essential for ensuring business continuity, maintaining customer trust, and protecting brand reputation. With a dynamic operating environment that often faces challenges such as food safety issues, negative publicity, and disruptions from unforeseen events, businesses need effective crisis management strategies. This chapter delves into handling food safety incidents, managing negative publicity, and creating a business continuity plan to ensure a proactive approach toward managing crises.

1. Handling Food Safety Incidents

Food safety is a critical concern in the food and beverage industry. Incidents of foodborne illnesses, contamination, and product recalls can harm customers, attract regulatory scrutiny, and damage a business's reputation. Prompt and effective handling of these incidents is essential.

Identifying and Isolating the Issue: The first step in managing a food safety crisis is identifying and isolating the source of contamination or hazard. Quick identification allows the business to prevent further harm and address the root cause.

Internal Safety Checks: Regular inspections, quality control checks, and rigorous food safety protocols help identify potential issues before they escalate. For example, routine temperature checks for perishable items or verifying ingredient sourcing for allergens can minimize risks.

Recall Procedures: In cases where products have already reached consumers, an effective recall process is essential. This includes identifying affected batches, notifying relevant stakeholders, and ensuring all recalled products are removed promptly.

Effective Communication During Incidents: Transparency is crucial when addressing food safety issues. Communicating with customers, employees, and regulators in a clear and timely manner can help contain the damage and maintain trust.

Public Statements and Apologies: If a contamination incident or foodborne illness occurs, businesses should issue an immediate public statement. Apologizing, explaining the steps being taken, and assuring customers that their safety is the top priority can help preserve trust.

Employee Communication: Employees should be informed of the issue, provided with guidelines on how to address customer questions, and trained on additional safety measures if needed.

Implementing Corrective Measures: Once the crisis has been addressed, corrective actions must be taken to prevent recurrence. These may involve refining safety protocols, investing in advanced quality control systems, or retraining staff.

Reviewing and Updating Safety Standards: Conducting a post-incident analysis helps pinpoint gaps in the current safety protocols. Implementing stricter checks, such as Hazard Analysis Critical Control Point (HACCP) plans, minimizes the risk of similar incidents.

Training and Audits: Training staff on safe handling practices and conducting regular food safety audits reinforces a culture of safety and accountability.

2. Managing Negative Publicity

Negative publicity can arise from various sources, such as unfavorable reviews, social media posts, or media coverage related to an incident. Swiftly addressing and managing negative publicity helps mitigate the damage to the brand's reputation.

Understanding the Source of Negative Publicity: Negative publicity may originate from legitimate complaints, misunderstandings, or, in some cases, misinformation. Identifying the source of the negative feedback allows the business to address the underlying issue effectively.

Monitoring Online and Media Mentions: Using tools to monitor reviews, social media, and news outlets for mentions of the brand enables quick responses to negative feedback.

Listening to Customer Feedback: Analyzing complaints can reveal patterns or specific areas of improvement, whether related to service quality, food safety, or customer experience.

Responding to Negative Feedback: A prompt and professional response to negative feedback can help contain damage and demonstrate a commitment to customer satisfaction. Engaging with the feedback can often turn a negative experience into a positive one.

Crafting a Thoughtful Response: When responding to public complaints, acknowledge the customer's concerns, apologize if necessary, and outline the steps being taken to resolve the issue. A personal, empathetic approach is more effective than a generic response.

Corrective Actions: Offering to rectify the situation, such as providing a refund, replacement, or discount, shows customers that their experience matters. For instance, if a customer had a negative experience due to delayed service, offering a free dessert or a future discount can encourage them to give the business another chance.

Engaging with Media: If negative publicity has spread to traditional media outlets, addressing the issue with transparency and professionalism is critical. Appointing a spokesperson, providing clear information, and being accessible to journalists demonstrate accountability.

Press Releases: Issuing a press release to explain the situation, outline corrective measures, and reaffirm the commitment to quality can help reshape public perception.

Crisis Communication Training: Preparing spokespersons and employees to handle media inquiries effectively reduces the risk of miscommunication during high-stress situations.

3. Business Continuity Planning

Business continuity planning (BCP) ensures that a business can operate through crises and recover quickly afterward. From supply chain disruptions to natural disasters, having a continuity plan in place helps minimize financial losses and operational impacts during unforeseen events.

Risk Assessment and Contingency Planning: Identifying potential risks and their impacts is the first step in creating a business continuity plan. Conducting a thorough risk assessment helps prioritize which areas require contingency plans.

Supply Chain Disruptions: In the event of disruptions in ingredient supply, alternative suppliers should be identified in advance. Building relationships with multiple suppliers for critical ingredients provides flexibility.

Infrastructure Risks: Natural disasters, fires, or equipment failures can disrupt operations. Implementing disaster preparedness measures, such as fire alarms, backup generators, and insurance, can help minimize losses.

Health Crises: During health crises, such as pandemics, businesses must have protocols in place to ensure customer and staff safety. Enhanced hygiene measures, social distancing policies, and options for contactless service help maintain operations.

Emergency Response Planning: The emergency response plan outlines specific actions to take in the immediate aftermath of a crisis. This includes evacuation procedures, customer and employee safety measures, and communication strategies.

Evacuation Procedures: In cases of fire or other emergencies, clearly defined evacuation routes and procedures ensure the safety of customers and staff.

Customer and Staff Communication: During a crisis, keeping everyone informed is essential. Training staff on emergency protocols and maintaining up-to-date customer contact information facilitates swift communication.

Post-Crisis Recovery: After a crisis, businesses must focus on recovery and restoration. The post-crisis phase involves assessing damage, implementing improvements, and communicating openly with customers and stakeholders.

Damage Assessment and Insurance Claims: Evaluating losses and submitting insurance claims helps recover financial stability. Documenting the impact of the crisis is essential for making accurate claims and understanding the full scope of damage.

Reputation Rebuilding: A post-crisis marketing campaign or public relations initiative can help restore customer trust. Highlighting any new improvements, such as upgraded safety protocols or renovations, reassures customers that the business has taken proactive steps to prevent future incidents.

Crisis management in the food and beverage industry is a proactive approach that helps protect businesses from potentially devastating situations. By implementing comprehensive food safety measures, addressing negative publicity with transparency, and establishing a robust business continuity plan, food and beverage businesses can navigate crises effectively and continue to thrive in the long term. Prioritizing customer safety, maintaining clear communication, and preparing for unexpected challenges enable businesses to uphold their reputation, foster customer loyalty, and ensure ongoing success despite setbacks.

Chapter 22: Emerging Technologies and Innovations

In recent years, the food and beverage industry has experienced a surge of technological advancements and innovations that are transforming traditional operations, enhancing customer experiences, and redefining how food and beverages are produced, delivered, and consumed. This chapter explores the role of the Internet of Things (IoT), automation, robotics, virtual kitchens, and ghost kitchens, as well as future trends that will likely shape the industry's evolution.

1. Role of IoT, Automation, and Robotics

The integration of IoT, automation, and robotics has brought significant efficiencies and improvements to the food and beverage industry, from kitchen operations to customer service.

Internet of Things (IoT): IoT is revolutionizing how businesses monitor, control, and manage various aspects of food production, storage, and distribution. IoT-enabled devices collect real-time data on everything from ingredient freshness to customer preferences, providing actionable insights that improve decision-making.

Inventory Management: IoT sensors can track inventory levels in real time, sending alerts when stock is low or when items near their expiration date. This minimizes waste and helps businesses keep essential items in stock without over-ordering.

Food Safety Monitoring: IoT devices can continuously monitor temperatures in refrigerators, freezers, and storage areas to ensure food is kept within safe temperature ranges. If temperatures fluctuate, alerts are automatically sent to staff, allowing them to address issues before food safety is compromised.

Predictive Maintenance: IoT sensors on kitchen equipment (e.g., ovens, fryers, dishwashers) monitor usage patterns and detect when maintenance is needed. Predictive maintenance reduces unexpected breakdowns, ensuring smooth operations and prolonging equipment lifespan.

Automation: Automation reduces labor-intensive tasks, speeds up processes, and enhances consistency across various operations. In the food and beverage industry, automation is utilized in food preparation, cooking, and service delivery.

Automated Food Preparation: Some kitchens use machines that can handle repetitive tasks like chopping, slicing, mixing, and even cooking. These systems ensure consistency and reduce the workload on human staff, allowing them to focus on more complex culinary tasks.

Order Processing: Digital ordering systems automate order processing, allowing for faster and more accurate fulfillment. Automated kiosks, for example, enable customers to place and pay for orders without staff assistance, reducing wait times.

Delivery Automation: Self-driving vehicles and drones are being tested for food delivery, offering the potential for faster and more efficient delivery services. Companies are also exploring robotic solutions for last-mile delivery in urban areas.

Robotics: Robots are making an impact in the food and beverage industry, especially in settings where precision, speed, and hygiene are paramount. Robotics enhances operational efficiency and provides unique customer experiences.

Food Preparation and Cooking: Robots equipped with culinary skills can cook a variety of dishes, from flipping burgers to crafting sushi. In fast-food establishments, robotic arms and automated fryers are being deployed to prepare food quickly and consistently.

Customer Service Robots: In some restaurants, robots are used as servers, delivering food to tables and interacting with customers. These robots reduce staff workload, enhance the customer experience, and offer a unique novelty that can attract patrons.

Cleaning and Sanitizing: Robots can clean floors, surfaces, and kitchen equipment efficiently, maintaining a high level of hygiene. During the COVID-19 pandemic, the demand for such robots increased, as they could perform tasks with minimal human intervention.

2. Virtual Kitchens and Ghost Kitchens

As customer preferences shift towards online ordering and food delivery, virtual kitchens and ghost kitchens have emerged as innovative solutions. These kitchens focus on fulfilling online orders without a dine-in option, reducing overhead costs and allowing businesses to operate more flexibly.

Understanding Virtual Kitchens and Ghost Kitchens: Virtual kitchens, also known as cloud kitchens or dark kitchens, are dedicated to preparing food for delivery services rather than in-house dining. They are designed to operate solely for online orders, reducing the need for physical space and traditional restaurant infrastructure.

Cost Savings and Efficiency: By eliminating dine-in areas, virtual kitchens reduce expenses on real estate, decor, and front-of-house staff. This allows restaurants to focus on the production of high-quality food and fast delivery, which can be especially advantageous in urban areas with high rent costs.

Flexible Menu Options: Virtual kitchens allow businesses to experiment with different concepts, cuisines, or brands under one roof. For instance, a kitchen might serve a variety of brands, each specializing in different cuisines (e.g., pizza, sushi, and tacos), thereby attracting a diverse customer base without the need for separate locations.

Data-Driven Decision Making: Virtual kitchens leverage data to optimize operations, menu offerings, and pricing strategies. By analyzing order trends, customer demographics, and popular items, these businesses can adapt their menus and processes to meet evolving customer demands.

Growth of the Ghost Kitchen Model: Ghost kitchens have gained traction as food delivery becomes increasingly popular. With a focus on logistics, they are equipped to handle high order volumes efficiently.

Partnerships with Delivery Services: Many ghost kitchens partner with third-party delivery platforms (such as UberEats, DoorDash, and Grubhub) to expand their reach and streamline order fulfillment.

Optimized Layout for High-Volume Production: Ghost kitchens are designed for maximum efficiency in food preparation and packing. Orders are processed in rapid succession, with minimal downtime between orders to ensure timely delivery.

Lowering Barriers to Entry: The ghost kitchen model allows entrepreneurs to enter the food and beverage industry with lower startup costs, as they do not need to invest in prime location real estate or customer seating areas. This model also allows established brands to expand to new locations with reduced risk.

3. Future Trends and Innovations on the Horizon

The food and beverage industry is continually evolving, and emerging technologies and consumer trends indicate a promising future filled with innovation. Some key trends to watch include:

Plant-Based and Alternative Proteins: Driven by increasing consumer awareness of sustainability and health, plant-based proteins and lab-grown meats are gaining popularity. Innovations in food science are enabling companies to create meat substitutes that closely mimic the texture, flavor, and appearance of traditional meat.

Alternative Proteins: Beyond plant-based products, lab-grown meat and insect-based proteins are emerging as viable protein sources. Companies are investing in research and development to make these proteins more accessible and appealing to mainstream consumers.

Sustainability and Ethical Considerations: With growing concerns about animal welfare and environmental impact, consumers are seeking alternatives to traditional animal-based products. This trend is expected to drive further innovation in sustainable food production.

Sustainable and Smart Packaging: Sustainability is influencing packaging trends, with businesses adopting eco-friendly materials and minimizing waste. Smart packaging, which integrates sensors and QR codes, also enhances customer engagement and provides transparency about product origins and ingredients.

Biodegradable and Recyclable Materials: The industry is increasingly moving towards packaging that is biodegradable, compostable, or recyclable. This shift reflects the growing consumer demand for environmentally responsible products.

Smart Packaging Features: Packaging that incorporates IoT technology can provide real-time information about product freshness, nutritional content, and ingredient sourcing. QR codes, for instance, can offer customers insights into a product's journey from farm to table.

Personalized and Data-Driven Dining Experiences: Data analytics and AI are enabling restaurants to provide personalized experiences, from tailored menu recommendations to targeted promotions.

AI-Powered Recommendation Systems: By analyzing customer order history, preferences, and demographics, AI algorithms can recommend dishes or suggest personalized meal plans. This approach enhances customer satisfaction and loyalty by catering to individual tastes.

Dynamic Pricing and Promotions: Using data to understand demand patterns, restaurants can adjust pricing, offer promotions, or tailor deals to increase sales. Dynamic pricing strategies optimize revenue by aligning with customer demand during peak and off-peak times.

Blockchain for Transparency and Traceability: Blockchain technology is being used to improve transparency across the supply chain, allowing customers to trace the origin of their food and verify sourcing claims.

Food Traceability: Blockchain enables end-to-end traceability by recording each stage of the supply chain, from farming to processing to delivery. This provides customers with confidence in the quality and authenticity of their food.

Enhanced Food Safety: By tracking food through every stage of the supply chain, blockchain can help prevent foodborne illnesses and identify contamination sources quickly, reducing recall time.

Conclusion

Emerging technologies and innovations in the food and beverage industry are reshaping traditional business models, improving efficiency, and catering to evolving customer expectations. From the Internet of Things and automation to virtual kitchens and sustainable packaging, these advancements are creating a more dynamic, responsive, and customer-focused industry. By staying informed about these trends, businesses can embrace innovation, improve their operations, and remain competitive in an ever-changing landscape. The future of the food and beverage industry promises to be an exciting blend of technology, sustainability, and personalized customer experiences.

Chapter 23: Food and Beverage Entrepreneurship

Starting a business in the food and beverage (F&B) industry can be an exciting and rewarding endeavor, but it also requires careful planning, an understanding of market dynamics, and a clear strategy for overcoming the challenges that new entrants often face. This chapter covers the essentials of launching an F&B business, from developing a business plan and securing funding to tackling the unique obstacles within this competitive industry.

1. How to Start a Food and Beverage Business

Launching a food and beverage business requires a combination of creativity, planning, and an understanding of the operational demands specific to this industry. Whether opening a restaurant, a food truck, or a packaged food company, these steps serve as a foundation.

Identify Your Niche and Concept: Choosing the right niche is essential in defining your brand and attracting a specific customer base. Options include opening a traditional or fast-casual restaurant, a coffee shop, a dessert bar, or even an online-only kitchen (ghost kitchen). Identifying a concept that resonates with your target audience will help differentiate you from competitors and attract loyal customers.

Market Research: Conducting thorough market research helps you understand customer preferences, existing competition, and emerging trends. Knowing your audience's dining preferences, income levels, and lifestyle will allow you to fine-tune your offerings to meet their needs effectively.

Choosing a Unique Selling Proposition (USP): Determine what will make your business stand out. Whether it's offering organic ingredients, unique recipes, or fast service, your USP should be clear and compelling to potential customers.

Develop Your Business Model: A well-defined business model is essential for planning your revenue streams, operating costs, and growth potential. Food and beverage businesses can adopt various models, from dine-in to delivery-only services.

Delivery and Takeout Model: With the rise of digital food delivery, consider whether your business will cater specifically to takeout and delivery customers, potentially reducing the need for expensive real estate and waitstaff.

Franchise or Independent Ownership: Decide if you want to start as an independent business or explore franchise opportunities. Franchising can be advantageous for entrepreneurs who prefer a proven concept, though it often involves royalties and restrictions on operational freedom.

Legal and Licensing Requirements: Compliance with food safety, health regulations, and business licenses is critical. Obtain the necessary permits for health, safety, and zoning, and ensure compliance with regulations around alcohol if you plan to serve it. Requirements vary by location, so research local regulations carefully to avoid costly fines or delays.

2. Business Planning and Securing Funding

Creating a comprehensive business plan and securing the necessary funding are vital steps in building a successful food and beverage business. These foundational elements provide direction, structure, and a roadmap to potential investors.

Crafting a Detailed Business Plan: A solid business plan outlines your vision, business structure, operational strategy, and financial projections.

This document is essential not only for guiding your efforts but also for convincing lenders or investors of the viability of your business.

Executive Summary: Start with an executive summary that succinctly explains your business concept, target market, and objectives. The summary should provide an overview of your company's purpose, mission, and goals.

Market Analysis: A market analysis section demonstrates your understanding of the competitive landscape. Include information on trends, customer demographics, and the potential demand for your offerings.

Marketing and Sales Strategy: Outline how you plan to attract and retain customers. This may include a description of your branding, digital marketing approach, and customer loyalty programs.

Financial Projections: Include a forecast of revenues, expenses, and cash flow for the first few years of operation. Show potential investors or lenders that your business can achieve profitability.

Securing Funding: Food and beverage businesses often require significant initial investment for rent, equipment, inventory, and staff. There are various funding options available, each with its pros and cons.

Self-Funding: Many entrepreneurs choose to use personal savings to start their businesses. This option gives you full control but also increases personal financial risk.

Bank Loans and Small Business Loans: Traditional bank loans and Small Business Administration (SBA) loans are popular choices for F&B startups. They often require collateral and a good credit history, as well as a detailed business plan.

Venture Capital and Angel Investors: For high-growth concepts with potential scalability, venture capital or angel investors can be a viable source of funding. However, these investors may expect equity or some degree of operational control.

Crowdfunding: Platforms like Kickstarter or GoFundMe allow entrepreneurs to secure small contributions from a large number of people. Crowdfunding can be an effective way to raise funds while building a loyal customer base early on.

Grants and Subsidies: In some regions, government programs and grants are available to support small businesses in the food sector. These funds can help with initial costs, provided you meet specific criteria.

3. Overcoming Challenges for New Entrants

The food and beverage industry is known for its competitive landscape and high failure rates among new businesses. Understanding the common challenges and implementing strategies to address them will increase your chances of success.

Managing Operating Costs: Labor, rent, and ingredient costs are major expenses in the F&B industry. Without careful management, these costs can erode profitability.

Labor Costs: Hiring and retaining skilled workers, from chefs to servers, can be challenging and costly. Cross-training staff, offering flexible scheduling, and creating an enjoyable work environment can help mitigate high turnover.

Ingredient Sourcing and Management: Establishing relationships with reliable suppliers is essential to securing quality ingredients at competitive prices. Monitoring inventory levels and reducing waste are also vital in controlling costs.

Lease and Utility Management: High lease rates in prime locations can strain finances. Consider locations that offer a balance between visibility and affordability or consider pop-up locations to test the market before committing to a lease.

Building Brand Loyalty: Customer loyalty is essential for repeat business, particularly in saturated markets. Focus on delivering consistent quality, exceptional customer service, and a unique experience.

Engaging Customer Service: Train staff to provide friendly, attentive service. Customer feedback and loyalty programs can also help foster a loyal customer base.

Personalization and Customer Engagement: Use technology to gather data on customer preferences, which can inform menu development and personalized promotions.

Brand Storytelling: A strong brand story can connect with customers emotionally. Sharing your journey, mission, or sustainability efforts can resonate with today's values-driven consumers.

Adapting to Market Trends: The food and beverage sector is influenced by trends such as health consciousness, sustainability, and digital transformation. Staying adaptable will help you remain relevant.

Health and Wellness Trends: Many consumers prioritize health-conscious options, including plant-based, organic, and gluten-free offerings. Regularly assess your menu to include healthier choices.

Sustainability: An increasing number of consumers are looking for environmentally responsible dining options. Implementing eco-friendly packaging, waste reduction strategies, and sustainable sourcing practices can attract these customers.

Digital and Online Presence: Online ordering and delivery have become essential for many F&B businesses. Invest in a user-friendly website, mobile ordering platform, and social media presence to engage customers and streamline operations.

Ensuring Compliance and Food Safety: Compliance with food safety and health regulations is paramount. Failing to meet standards can lead to penalties, legal issues, and reputational damage.

Implementing Robust Food Safety Protocols: Develop and maintain food safety protocols that cover cleanliness, temperature control, and handling procedures. These protocols protect your customers and your reputation.

Training Staff on Health and Safety: Regularly train staff on hygiene standards and proper food handling. Certifications such as the Hazard Analysis and Critical Control Points (HACCP) can demonstrate your commitment to safety.

Dealing with Inspections and Audits: Health inspections can be stressful for new businesses, but thorough preparation will help you pass them confidently. Regularly review local regulations to stay updated on requirements.

Starting a food and beverage business requires strategic planning, a deep understanding of market dynamics, and the agility to adapt to industry trends and challenges. A clear business plan, adequate funding, and proactive strategies for managing costs and building brand loyalty are essential components of success. By embracing innovation, focusing on customer satisfaction, and maintaining rigorous compliance standards, entrepreneurs can thrive in this vibrant and dynamic industry.

Chapter 24: Case Studies of Successful Food and Beverage Brands

Examining the successes and failures of established food and beverage (F&B) companies provides invaluable lessons for aspiring entrepreneurs. This chapter profiles several leading F&B brands, explores the key strategies behind their achievements, and highlights how certain ventures have stumbled, offering crucial insights into the complex dynamics of the industry.

1. Profiles of Leading F&B Companies and Brands

Exploring the strategies of leading F&B brands gives insight into how different approaches—from innovation and branding to supply chain management—contribute to long-term success.

McDonald's: As one of the largest and most recognizable fast-food brands globally, McDonald's success is attributed to its focus on consistency, branding, and operational efficiency.

Operational Efficiency: McDonald's pioneered the "Speedee Service System," a production-line approach to food preparation, which drastically improved service speed and consistency.

Franchise Model: By expanding through franchising, McDonald's scaled rapidly without massive capital investments and created an ecosystem where franchisees are incentivized to adhere to quality and brand standards.

Adaptability: McDonald's has adapted its menu in various regions to cater to local tastes and dietary restrictions, such as offering vegetarian options in India and ramen burgers in Japan. This flexibility strengthens its global appeal.

Starbucks: Starbucks transformed coffee culture worldwide and created a unique experience around its product.

Customer Experience: Starbucks emphasized creating a "third place" between home and work where customers could relax, study, or meet friends. The ambiance and store layout became integral parts of the brand identity.

Employee Training and Empowerment: Starbucks invests heavily in employee training, which has contributed to high customer service standards and loyalty. Employee benefits also improve retention and align staff with the brand's values.

Digital Innovation: Starbucks' mobile app and loyalty program are cornerstones of its success, allowing for digital ordering, payment, and rewards tracking. These innovations have increased convenience, customer engagement, and brand loyalty.

Nestlé: A giant in the global food industry, Nestlé's success highlights the importance of product diversification and an integrated supply chain.

Product Portfolio: Nestlé has a diverse range of products, from bottled water and infant nutrition to pet care. This wide portfolio helps mitigate risk by spreading revenue sources across different product categories and markets.

Sustainability Initiatives: Nestlé has made substantial efforts in sustainability, committing to ethical sourcing and reducing plastic waste. These initiatives improve its brand reputation and align with the increasing consumer demand for sustainable practices.

Global Reach with Local Focus: Nestlé has a presence in over 190 countries but tailors its products to meet local preferences and regulatory requirements, balancing global reach with local customization.

Domino's Pizza: Known for its dominance in the pizza delivery market, Domino's success can be attributed to its tech-driven approach and strong focus on customer convenience.

Digital Transformation: Domino's leveraged technology early on, offering a seamless online ordering experience and tracking options for deliveries. Its digital initiatives have significantly boosted sales and made it one of the most accessible brands in the pizza delivery market.

Customer Engagement: Through creative marketing, such as the "Domino's Tracker," the brand fosters a sense of transparency and engagement. Domino's Tracker allows customers to monitor their orders, which enhances the experience and builds customer trust.

Rapid Response to Feedback: Domino's showed adaptability by responding to customer criticism in 2010 about the quality of its pizza. By reformulating its recipe and launching a transparent marketing campaign, Domino's turned customer feedback into an opportunity for positive brand transformation.

2. Lessons from Successful and Failed Ventures

Success in the F&B industry often depends on various factors, including customer experience, product quality, marketing, and financial management. However, for each successful venture, there are also stories of businesses that failed to navigate market challenges.

Success Stories

Chipotle Mexican Grill: Known for its commitment to "Food with Integrity," Chipotle built a unique brand focused on fresh, responsibly sourced ingredients. Its focus on transparency and quality has helped it maintain customer loyalty, despite challenges like food safety incidents.

Ben & Jerry's: This ice cream brand stands out for its strong brand values, commitment to social causes, and creative product offerings. Ben & Jerry's has successfully differentiated itself by championing sustainability, fair trade, and progressive social issues, attracting loyal customers who align with these values.

Shake Shack: Originally a hotdog cart in New York, Shake Shack has grown into a popular fast-casual burger chain. Shake Shack focuses on premium ingredients, quality service, and a "fun" brand experience. Its emphasis on fresh ingredients and a high-quality product differentiates it from many fast-food competitors.

Learning from Failures

Krispy Kreme: Though initially successful, Krispy Kreme's rapid expansion in the early 2000s led to financial instability. By opening too many stores and franchises too quickly, the brand struggled with debt and declining demand in oversaturated markets. The key lesson here is the importance of sustainable growth over rapid, uncontrolled expansion.

Boston Market: Despite its initial popularity, Boston Market faced financial challenges due to over-expansion, high operating costs, and lack of differentiation. The brand struggled to compete with fast-casual chains offering healthier or more customizable options. Boston Market's experience highlights the risks of ignoring changing consumer preferences and failing to innovate.

Sears' Restaurant Division: Sears tried to enter the food and beverage market by opening in-store restaurants. However, this strategy failed due to a lack of focus and misalignment with the core retail business. This failure illustrates the importance of staying true to one's brand identity and not diluting resources by branching into unrelated industries.

3. Key Takeaways for Aspiring F&B Entrepreneurs

Analyzing both successes and failures offers several critical takeaways for aspiring entrepreneurs:

Focus on Core Values and Consistency: Brands like McDonald's and Starbucks maintain consistent values and quality across all locations. For new businesses, defining core values and maintaining consistency in product and service can build trust and loyalty.

Prioritize Customer Experience: Many successful brands go beyond the product itself to focus on the overall customer experience. This includes elements such as store ambiance, digital interactions, and personalized service, which all contribute to a memorable customer journey.

Adaptability and Innovation are Key: As seen with Domino's digital transformation and Chipotle's ingredient transparency, adaptability is crucial in the F&B industry. The ability to embrace technology and respond to customer feedback keeps brands relevant and competitive.

Sustainable Growth: Over-expansion can harm businesses, as shown by Krispy Kreme and Boston Market. Growth should be strategic, with careful consideration given to each new location, to avoid market saturation and financial strain.

Brand Differentiation: With high competition, new entrants must offer something unique. Whether it's a distinctive menu, ethical sourcing, or innovative customer engagement, establishing a strong brand identity differentiates a business in the marketplace.

Listen to Customer Feedback: Successful brands often treat feedback as a tool for improvement. Domino's transparent approach to revamping its pizza based on customer criticism is an example of how turning negative feedback into positive action can help a brand grow stronger.

Financial Discipline and Planning: Managing costs, cash flow, and resources is essential. Failed ventures often suffer from poor financial management and lack of realistic budgeting. A solid financial foundation and cost control are critical for navigating the ups and downs of the F&B industry.

Build a Strong Team and Culture: Starbucks and Ben & Jerry's emphasize employee training, empowerment, and a positive work culture. Creating a cohesive, well-trained team is essential, as employees are often the direct interface between customers and the brand.

Stay Attuned to Trends: Successful F&B brands are quick to adopt emerging trends, whether they relate to health, sustainability, or technology. A proactive approach to trends allows businesses to stay relevant and meet the evolving preferences of their customers.

Case studies of successful F&B brands offer a wealth of insights into the strategies, challenges, and best practices that underpin lasting success in the food and beverage industry. By understanding both the achievements and mistakes of established brands, aspiring entrepreneurs can build a foundation for success, emphasizing brand consistency, customer experience, adaptability, and financial discipline. With these principles in mind, new entrants can better navigate the complex but rewarding world of food and beverage entrepreneurship.

Chapter 25: Future of the Food and Beverage Industry

The food and beverage (F&B) industry is undergoing rapid transformations driven by technological advancements, shifts in consumer preferences, and the urgent need for sustainable practices. This chapter explores predicted changes and trends, the growing role of technology and sustainability, and the opportunities and challenges that await the next generation of F&B entrepreneurs and professionals.

1. Predicted Industry Changes and Trends

Several trends are reshaping the F&B landscape, impacting everything from product offerings to how food is produced and consumed.

Plant-Based and Alternative Proteins: As consumers become increasingly aware of the environmental impact of traditional livestock farming, demand for plant-based and alternative protein sources, such as lab-grown meat, is expected to continue growing. Companies like Beyond Meat and Impossible Foods have led the way, inspiring both startups and established brands to invest in meat alternatives.

Personalized Nutrition: Advances in data collection and biotechnology are making personalized nutrition more accessible. DNA-based dietary recommendations, apps that track health and eating patterns, and customized meal plans are becoming increasingly popular. As consumers seek food that aligns with their specific health goals, the F&B industry is likely to see a rise in tailored offerings that cater to individual dietary needs.

Functional Foods and Beverages: Health-conscious consumers are driving demand for functional foods and beverages that offer additional health benefits. Products containing ingredients like probiotics, adaptogens, and vitamins are popular among consumers looking for items that support wellness. This trend is expected to expand as more people turn to food as a way to enhance their physical and mental health.

Transparency and Ethical Sourcing: Consumers are increasingly interested in knowing where their food comes from and how it's produced. This trend has fueled demand for transparency and ethical sourcing, pushing companies to provide detailed information about the origins and practices behind their products. Ethical considerations, including animal welfare and fair labor practices, are also influencing purchasing decisions.

Rise of "Ghost Kitchens" and Virtual Brands: The shift towards delivery and takeout, accelerated by the COVID-19 pandemic, has led to the rise of ghost kitchens—kitchens that exclusively prepare food for delivery. Virtual brands that operate without physical storefronts are also emerging, reducing costs and maximizing reach through digital platforms. This model is expected to continue as it offers scalability and flexibility in the changing market.

2. Role of Technology and Sustainability

The F&B industry is leveraging new technologies to improve efficiency, enhance customer experience, and address sustainability challenges.

Automation and Robotics: Automation is transforming operations, especially in repetitive tasks like food preparation, cooking, and packaging. Robotics is being introduced in areas such as salad preparation, drink dispensing, and order delivery, reducing labor costs and ensuring consistency. In large-scale operations, automation allows for faster production while minimizing human error.

Internet of Things (IoT): IoT enables real-time monitoring and data collection throughout the supply chain, from tracking food safety parameters to optimizing inventory management. Sensors and smart devices can monitor food temperature, freshness, and inventory levels, alerting staff when action is needed. This technology enhances safety, reduces waste, and ensures that products meet quality standards.

Blockchain for Transparency: Blockchain technology offers an immutable record of transactions, making it possible to trace food products from farm to table. This is especially important in cases of contamination or fraud. By ensuring transparency, blockchain can help build consumer trust and make it easier for companies to prove the integrity of their sourcing practices.

Sustainable Packaging Innovations: The push to reduce plastic waste has led to innovative solutions in sustainable packaging. From biodegradable materials and edible packaging to compostable containers, companies are exploring alternatives to single-use plastics. The development of sustainable packaging not only meets consumer demand but also aligns with environmental goals.

Artificial Intelligence (AI) and Data Analytics: AI and data analytics are revolutionizing decision-making in the F&B industry. From demand forecasting to menu optimization, AI algorithms analyze consumer data to identify trends, anticipate demand, and personalize customer interactions. AI-driven insights allow companies to be more responsive to customer preferences and optimize their operations.

Sustainable Sourcing and Regenerative Agriculture: As awareness of climate change grows, F&B companies are adopting sustainable sourcing practices and supporting regenerative agriculture, which aims to restore soil health and biodiversity. Regenerative agriculture not only benefits the environment but also enhances food quality, making it a priority for many F&B brands.

3. Opportunities and Challenges for the Next Generation

The future of the F&B industry presents exciting opportunities, but also significant challenges that will require innovative solutions and a proactive mindset.

Opportunities

Expansion of Alternative Foods: With the growing interest in plant-based proteins and alternative foods, there are ample opportunities for innovation in product development. Entrepreneurs can explore new ingredients, flavor profiles, and processing methods to create alternatives that appeal to diverse consumer tastes.

Direct-to-Consumer (DTC) Models: DTC models have become more viable with the growth of e-commerce and delivery services. By connecting directly with consumers, F&B companies can bypass traditional retail channels, build closer relationships with customers, and capture valuable data for personalized marketing.

Growth of Digital Ordering and Delivery: The demand for convenience is driving the expansion of digital ordering and delivery platforms. New entrants can capitalize on this trend by developing unique food concepts suited to the delivery model, such as virtual brands or innovative packaging that maintains food quality.

Focus on Sustainability and Social Impact: Consumers are rewarding brands that demonstrate a commitment to sustainability and social responsibility. Startups that prioritize eco-friendly practices and ethical sourcing will appeal to environmentally conscious consumers, creating new avenues for market differentiation.

Emerging Market Expansion: Rapid urbanization and a growing middle class in emerging markets are driving demand for F&B products. These markets offer untapped opportunities for companies willing to adapt their offerings to local tastes and preferences.

Challenges

Navigating Complex Regulations: Compliance with food safety, labeling, and environmental regulations is becoming increasingly complex, especially for businesses operating across borders. The next generation of F&B entrepreneurs will need to stay informed and agile to navigate regulatory changes.

Managing Rising Costs: Costs for raw materials, labor, and transportation are rising, which can impact profitability. Inflation and supply chain disruptions also add to the financial pressures. Companies will need to find ways to optimize their operations and manage costs without compromising quality.

Addressing Climate Change: As one of the largest contributors to greenhouse gas emissions, the F&B industry faces pressure to adopt sustainable practices that reduce its environmental footprint. Companies that fail to take action may face consumer backlash or regulatory fines.

Competition in a Crowded Market: The F&B industry is highly competitive, with new brands entering the market every day. To stand out, businesses will need to offer unique value propositions, such as exceptional customer experiences, innovative products, or sustainable practices.

Adapting to Consumer Demands: Today's consumers are more health-conscious, environmentally aware, and digitally savvy. Meeting their demands requires constant innovation and the flexibility to adapt to emerging trends, which can be challenging for companies with established practices.

Conclusion

The future of the F&B industry is shaped by dynamic forces, including technological advancement, sustainability imperatives, and evolving consumer preferences. From personalized nutrition to sustainable packaging and AI-driven insights, the industry is being redefined by the need for innovation and responsibility.

For the next generation of F&B entrepreneurs, success will depend on staying attuned to these trends and anticipating changes. Those who embrace technology, prioritize sustainability, and understand the shifting values of consumers will be best positioned to thrive in a rapidly changing landscape. The path forward offers rich opportunities for those ready to navigate the challenges of an industry that is central to daily life, culture, and the global economy.

www.ingramcontent.com/pod-product-compliance
Lightning Source LLC
Chambersburg PA
CBHW071125240526
45465CB00024B/1098